RACING POST

HORSERACING
Miscellany

*Marvellous, Miscellaneous
Moments from 400 Years of
Horseracing History*

GRAHAM SHARPE

First published by Pitch Publishing,
for and on behalf of the Racing Post, 2022

RACING POST

Racing Post
9 Donnington Park,
85 Birdham Road,
Chichester,
West Sussex,
PO20 7AJ
www.pitchpublishing.co.uk
info@pitchpublishing.co.uk

ISBN 978 1 83950 107 4

Typesetting and origination by Racing Post

Printed and bound in Great Britain by TJ Books, Padstow

Contents

Introduction

I have been racing in many parts of the world since, as barely – if at all – a teenager, I first sat on Glorious Goodwood's Trundle Hill to watch the racing action happening below, for free, back in the early 1960s.

As I began to become a regular racegoer, it didn't take me long to realise that there is virtually always something to be seen or heard for the first time, wherever and whenever I attend.

Working in and around racing for almost half a century, and visiting many tracks abroad in Europe and beyond, I collected and stored racecourse stories galore, many of them personally experienced.

In Switzerland it was the heroic male figure stepping confidently out on to the racecourse, arms aloft, to capture a runner that had shed its jockey and was running free. The unimpressed horse just galloped straight over macho man, to the delight of the crowd.

In Germany, at Baden-Baden's Iffezheim course, where they have raced since 1858, I saw Elvis Presley acting as the starter. In Guernsey at the island's L'Ancresse course (a golf course every other day of the year), the starter used a set of kitchen steps as his rostrum.

In Australia, at Flemington, I witnessed the Japanese owners of the Melbourne Cup winner, taking their trophy away on a local train, surrounded by tipsy Aussie racegoers (there didn't seem to be any other type!).

In Sweden a race horse gave me an each-way tip, which profitably finished second at 12-1.

Such quirky occurrences are a great part of horseracing. Every racegoer has experienced something out of the ordinary – a humorous, unexpected, outrageous, hilarious, amazing, baffling, bizarre incident – and hundreds of them appear in the pages of this small but perfectly formed volume of miscellaneous turf tales and racecourse romps, for your equine edification and entertainment.

Graham Sharpe
Racegoer, punter and author

Horseracing in the pandemic

The Grand National – together with the rest of the Aintree meeting – was called off on 16 March 2020 as a result of the Covid-19 pandemic.

* * *

The Cheltenham Festival, which had just finished, had completed all four days of the meeting, with bumper crowds – albeit slightly below the previous year's turnout.

'In some ways, I would say that this has been a wonderful distraction before we face the reality of what the next month or so may have in store for us. It's been a great four days' racing and a wonderful release for an awful lot of people,' said Cheltenham chief Ian Renton, summing up the 2020 festival, which faced widespread criticism for taking place while almost all other major sporting fixtures were being postponed or cancelled as the threat of coronavirus kicked in.

'There has been an overriding sense of the band continuing to play as the *Titanic* goes down about this year's festival,' wrote Marcus Armytage of the *Daily Telegraph*, nailing the bizarre atmosphere of Cheltenham in 2020, while Greg Wood of *The Guardian* wasn't disagreeing, 'Racing tends to live in its own little world at the best of times – for many that is part of the attraction – but the sense of deliberate detachment can never have felt so strong.'

'Many of those breezing into Cheltenham this week may have thought they were tapping into a form of Dunkirk spirit, but the sceptics would deem *dummkopf* a more fitting term and wonder if any celebration of horses, alcohol and gambling was worth this risk,' wrote *The Times*'s Rick Broadbent on 14 March, seeming to sit on the fence in wondering whether Cheltenham should have taken place.

'If Cheltenham was being held in Ireland I don't think it would be on, quite frankly,' *The Times* quoted Ireland's minister for foreign affairs, Simon Coveney, that same day.

Eight days earlier, a public health notice posted on the British Horseracing Authority's website had implored people, 'Do not travel to the festival if you have any of the following symptoms – a cough, high temperature or shortness of breath AND you have been to, or transited through the high-risk countries, or been in contact with anyone that has in the last 14 days.'

* * *

Paddy Power announced they would be closing all their betting shops in Britain from Friday, 20 March until the end of April as the UK government confirmed it had asked a range of businesses such as cafes, pubs and restaurants to close as a result of the pandemic.

* * *

Opening the ITV4 coverage of Irish racing from Thurles in County Tipperary on Saturday, 21 March, presenter Ed Chamberlin told viewers, 'Sport is trivial at a time when the world is a grim place, but we want today's live racing to offer those who are suffering a small tonic.'

Then, as the show closed after showing five races, commentator Richard Hoiles hit just the right tone as he signed off, saying, 'By definition our audience is generally elderly … if you're of that demographic, you're facing an extremely worrying time. A lot of you have supported racing right through since the initial ITV era. To be faced with the chance of going into seclusion for a long period of time – Brough [Scott] was saying he's not able to see his grandkids at the moment – it must be particularly difficult.

'Loads [of elderly people] work at racecourses – I nod at car park attendants, and people who work in the weighing room. I don't know names.

'Thank you for your support of the sport and hopefully if we can continue even in small measure just to give you some brief glimpse of normality, then hopefully it's just helping you out in what's a very difficult time.'

Metro newspaper racing correspondent Nick Metcalfe called the programme 'one of the most unusual sports broadcasts any of us can remember seeing on British television.'

* * *

On Sunday, 22 March, six days before it was due to happen, the Dubai World Cup meeting at Meydan was called off on health grounds.

Trainer Charlie Fellowes questioned the timing of the cancellation, having sent his globetrotting yard favourite Prince Of Arran to the United Arab Emirates just two days earlier.

Fellowes had planned to run the seven-year-old in the Dubai Gold Cup after being given assurance that the meeting would take place behind closed doors.

'If we'd had an inkling that this was going to happen we wouldn't have sent the horse with the other Europeans on Friday.

Quite why they left it this late to call it off I don't know, but the decision obviously transcends racing,' he said.

Golden Slipper won the Hong Kong Derby by a neck from outsider Playa Del Puente in a spectacular last-to-first finish on Sunday, 22 March at Sha Tin, where the meeting took place behind closed doors.

Respected leading jumps trainer Nicky Henderson said of how the crisis was affecting him and his counterparts, 'We've been a lucky generation, as we're the first that's not had to have a ghastly experience of a world war. We've been relatively crisis-free. We had the Falklands War, we had foot and mouth disease and we took all those seriously, but this far outweighs any of those.'

Kieren Fallon was a winner in the saddle but had to admit defeat when confronted with panic-buying at his local supermarket, reported David Milnes to *Racing Post* readers on 23 March.

The six-time champion jockey had tried to stock up after returning from a winter spell riding out in Dubai but was left stunned by what greeted him in the shopping aisles of West Suffolk.

The three-time Derby winner told Milnes, 'I was still on Dubai time, four hours ahead, when I got back so it was no problem to get up early and get over to Tesco in Bury St Edmunds around 7am. Everything appeared quiet, but before I knew it, people just appeared like locusts and there was nothing left that anyone wanted. I've never seen anything like it. It's certainly not like that in Dubai, so it was a bit of a shock to the system.

'I then tried a nearby Aldi on the way home but they were queuing out of the door at 7.30am. I managed to get some supplies in Newmarket Tesco on Saturday morning, but there was no pasta and baked beans were scarce.'

Racing Post editor Tom Kerr told readers on 25 March, 'It is with great sadness I must announce that following Thursday's edition the *Racing Post* will be temporarily suspending publication. Unfortunately, with racing in Britain and Ireland halted, betting shops closed, and our governments urging everyone to stay at home as much as possible to slow the spread of the coronavirus, we have been left with no other choice.

'Recent events have had an unfathomable impact on our world. We have seen harrowing pictures of overcrowded hospitals and overwhelmed medical professionals in other countries, and in Britain and Ireland we are bracing ourselves for similar scenes, while hoping the extensive measures announced thus far will forestall them.

'Sport and betting pale into insignificance when weighed against such terrible events, but we hope in these difficult last two weeks we have provided our readers with the information they need to understand what is happening, and some welcome distraction from the unrelenting news about Covid-19's spread. In particular, I hope we have helped keep those employed in racing and facing difficult financial times ahead informed about the support available to them.'

Christophe Soumillon, one of the most successful and most travelled jockeys in the world for the past two decades, expressed horror at being allowed back into France, one of the worst-affected countries in Europe, without being tested for coronavirus.

The 38-year-old was quoted in a story dated 25 March as saying he had 'more trouble at the bakery than at customs' when he arrived at Paris's Charles De Gaulle Airport as he returned from Dubai after the cancellation of the previous weekend's Dubai World Cup meeting, according to horseracingplanet.com.

'In the past month, I travelled a lot in Dubai, Hong Kong and Japan,' he said in an interview with the *Super Moscato Show* on France's RMC radio station. 'Since the start of the epidemic, I have done several tests, all negative, so as not to bring the virus home.

'This Monday morning, arriving at customs, I was shocked. I did not undergo any control. I find it absurd. They did not take the temperature, and they asked me nothing, neither email address nor telephone number.'

Newly crowned champion jump jockey – the first time since 1995 that neither A.P. McCoy or Richard Johnson had won the title – Brian Hughes, 34, with 141 winners, was disappointed that the season had been cut short because of coronavirus, but commented, 'There is a global crisis, and racing is not that important in the grand scheme of things.'

He was philosophical about racing having stopped, 'God forbid if someone got seriously injured when the NHS is as stretched and busy as it is.' He also stopped riding out, 'You try and do your bit for the country by staying at home.'

Racing Characters

BENNY ANDERSSON

ABBA's Benny Andersson has also made a name for himself on the horseracing scene. His stable is referred to as Chess Racing, and his most recent useful recruit was Lavender's Blue, who won first time out at Newmarket in April 2019 and went on to clock up £190,000 of prize money before the end of 2021.

Robert Havlin rode the filly to her first victory, sporting Benny's racing colours of black and silver checks.

Lavender's Blue's goal was to take on the elite in the Oaks at Epsom on 31 May, which she did, albeit finishing unplaced.

Benny Andersson has raced with several generations of Lavender's Blue's family. In the 1990s, he bought her granddam, Mondschein, who won in England and France.

Mondschein's offspring were also successful. Sibelius won the Danish Derby in 2004 and Ray won when the new race track Bro Park in Stockholm, was opened in 2016.

Her best offspring was Lavender's Blue's dam, Beatrice Aurore, who competed at Group level in England, France, Italy and Ireland.

Interviewed by the *Racing Post*'s Howard Wright in 2008, Benny reflected, 'It's always best to remember that the most common thing in racing is that your horse doesn't win. I didn't get involved in horseracing and breeding for recognition or success. It just grabbed me. I was fascinated by all the data and books about great race horses and trainers.

'If there's a race to win in this world, it's the Arc [Prix de l'Arc de Triomphe]. I might never do it, but if you're not in the game, how can you possibly win anything? I'm not giving up yet.

'The Arc is even more competitive than the Derby, because it's not just for three-year-olds and it's run at the time of year when most horses have gone to bed, so it takes a tough one to win. But I still wouldn't mind winning the Derby!'

Benny DID win the Derby – albeit the Danish Derby, with the musically named Sibelius.

He says he has no problem with others naming their horses after ABBA songs, but doesn't intend doing so himself. That has happened, with the likes of Dancing Queen, who never won; I Have A Dream, a name used for horses in several countries, producing a French winner.

Mamma Mia failed to win in Ireland, and Super Trouper did not fare much better, while a British-trained Voulez Vous did not manage to win.

BURT BACHARACH

Cigar won the inaugural World Cup in Dubai in 1996 when it was run at Nad Al Sheba. Finishing second on a night when American horses occupied the first three places was Soul of the Matter, owned and bred in West Virginia by composer Burt Bacharach's Blue Seas Music, and carrying his powder blue silks with musical notes on the back.

For a moment, as Cigar and Soul of the Matter came down the stretch, it looked like Bacharach and trainer Richard Mandella might upset Cigar, but it wasn't to be, and Soul of the Matter was second, beaten by a mere half a length.

Bacharach was there that day and he and wife Jane danced the night away under the Dubai moonlight as the band entertaining the World Cup guests played some of the most famous tunes from the Bacharach – and composing partner, Hal – David songbook.

Soul of the Matter was retired to stud. Just before this, in late June 1996, the songwriter's very useful Afternoon Deelites suffered a tendon injury that also meant the end of his racing career. Burt was philosophical, 'You know these things can happen, you hold your breath every time, but you don't think you'll get the double punch that quick.'

Burt's initial venture into ownership happened in 1968, when he asked Hall of Fame trainer Charlie Whittingham to find him a horse, and Battle Royal won for him first time out, whetting the songwriter's appetite for the sport.

Burt's Heartlight No. One, a three-yer-old filly named after a hit collaboration with Neil Diamond, also did well for him in 1983. Bacharach continued to own horses, albeit none reaching the heights that Soul of the Matter and Afternoon Deelites did.

Following a 2017 fire at San Luis Rey Downs in Bonsall, California, which claimed the lives of 47 horses and left several people injured, Bacharach teamed up with Elvis Costello, Anjelica Huston, and Bo Derek for a fundraiser to benefit those affected.

RACHAEL BLACKMORE

'I don't feel male, I don't feel female right now – I don't even feel human!' declared an emotional Rachael Blackmore after riding her 11-1, 11-year-old partner Minella Times in what had just become the first Grand National won by a female jockey, on 10 April 2021.

The horse was trained by Henry de Bromhead – who had, amazingly enough, also saddled the runner-up, Balko des Flos, after he had also recently won the big three races at the Cheltenham Festival – resulting in a £2,053.30 Exacta and £882.65 Computer Straight Forecast payout.

Rachael's triumph came shortly after she had stunned the racing world as she was leading jockey at the 2021 Cheltenham Festival, sadly bereft of spectators as a result of Covid restrictions.

Alastair Down informed *Racing Post* readers of his thoughts about Rachael, 'Out on course she is ruthless – part piranha and part striking cobra.'

Born on 11 July 1989, Rachael, daughter of Eimir and Charles, a teacher and a farmer, grew up on a dairy farm in Killenaule, Tipperary. Charles bred horses and she grew up riding them on the farm in Mortlestown Castle, getting her first horse, Bubbles, at the age of seven. She was soon riding at pony club events, hunting and pony racing.

Academically, she achieved a degree in equine science from the University of Limerick and reportedly had set her sights on becoming a vet – but at the same time she was working on that she was riding out and taking part in races as an amateur.

'I'm 71 – and it's one of the great achievements in sport I have lived to see. It's gigantic,' declared a parent who should know – Ted Walsh, father of jockeys Ruby and Katie on Rachael's Grand National win.

Former *Woman's Hour* presenter Jenni Murray was also keen to praise Rachael after the National: 'Thank you for proving me right, when I said a woman could win the Grand National. It's the only race I ever bet on and you won me £65 – my best win since 1983 when Jenny Pitman advised me to back Corbiere.'

In mid-April 2021, Rachael sat down with another racing great, Katie Walsh, for a quickfire question session, tweeted by the Jockey Club in which Katie threw options at her.

Tea or coffee? 'I don't drink tea or coffee. I know it's very unsocial when you go to someone's house … then they ask do you want a mineral water? I don't drink fizzy drinks, so I end up getting a glass of water.'

Snow or sun? 'Snow.'

Horses or dogs? 'Horses.'

Gold Cup or Grand National? 'Gold Cup.'

Punchestown or Cheltenham? 'Cheltenham.'

Ruby or A.P.? 'Ruby.'

TV series or film? 'Film.'

Red Rum or Tiger Roll? 'Tiger Roll.'

Songs certain to get you on the dance floor? 'Anything kind of hardcore r'n'b.'

If you weren't a jockey what would you be doing? 'I'd be still in college trying to be a vet.'

Three things you don't leave the house without? 'My phone, my keys – I don't like walking anywhere, and in the morning I take Nutella and pitta bread with me in the car.'

Top Irish jockey Davy Russell first recommended 21-year-old conditional jockey Rachael to trainer Shark Hanlon for a horse called Stowaway Pearl in a Thurles handicap hurdle in February 2011.

But she was unaware that, as Russell later revealed, 'We were having a couple of quid on the horse and I didn't wish to inform her.' He revealed in a March 2021 interview that he had told her, 'When you're crossing the top, kick and don't look back.' She did, eventually have a sneaky peek back – and found she was 15 lengths clear.

Hanlon played a huge part in setting Blackmore on her way. 'She rode her very first bumper winner for me, her very first obstacle winner for me, her first chase winner and her very first point-to-point winner,' he said.

'She was always a great lady, always really devoted, and a great employee, unbelievable. She had a lot of capability and I understood she had it and she had the heart to strive. That's what got her where she is, and she's hardy, she doesn't mind the falls. I found she was unreal at getting horses to leap. That was one of her huge, big plusses for me and I'd state for everybody else now.'

Rachael turned pro in March 2015, having ridden 11 point-to-point winners and seven as an amateur rider.

In 2021 she finished with six festival winners across the four days, becoming the first female jockey to win the Ruby Walsh Trophy for leading Cheltenham jockey.

In 2022 she and Honeysuckle teamed up yet again as they maintained the horse's unbeaten run and completed a Champion Hurdle double. The crowds roared again as the pair walked in after the race.

Rachael was soon back out contesting her next race. This time it didn't go quote as well. Sports writer Paul Hayward observed,

'Forty minutes after winning the Champion Hurdle, Blackmore hit the deck so hard after a fall from Telmesomethinggirl that her body bounced off the turf like a beachball.'

After winning the Grand National, Rachael's profile soared – and it must have been one of her finest achievements, given her background, that she also became the official face of Tipperary Fresh Milk!

But on Friday, 18 March 2022, Rachael probably exceeded even her Champion Hurdle high when she and A Plus Tard, the 3-1 favourite, went one better than the previous year to win the Gold Cup, and stifle the demons from her runner-up performance on the same horse in 2021, 'I knew coming down to the last this year that I had more horse underneath me. When I landed I gave him a squeeze and he picked up and I knew I was going to gallop all the way to the line, but you don't truly believe it until you cross the line. I've had so many special days. I wouldn't swap the Grand National for anything … but this is the Gold Cup.'

But she remains aware that jockeys are seldom more than a race away from a potentially career- – or even life – ending incident.

WINSTON CHURCHILL

One of England's greatest figures, Winston Churchill, born in 1874, was a keen racing man. He owned a very useful chaser called Colonist II who, at the end of the 1940s and beginning of the 1950s, won 13 races for him, worth some £120,000 in prize money.

But he also rode in races – and found himself mixed up in a scandal when a race, in which he had finished third, was alleged to have been crooked.

Having finished runner-up in a March 1895 steeplechase in which he almost broke a leg as his mount refused and swerved, leaving him 'bruised and very stiff', Churchill recovered quickly and a few days later was lining up to take part in the 4th Hussars Subalterns' Challenge Cup, finishing third.

'It was very exciting and there is no doubt about it being dangerous,' he said. 'I had never jumped a regulation fence before.'

However, there was a shock after the race when it was declared void with allegations having been made that the winner was a ringer, and that 'all those in the race must have been in on the plot'.

A publication called *Truth* declared, 'The coup resulted in the defeat of a hot favourite by the last outsider in the betting.'

Churchill declared himself outraged by the allegations and urged his mother to take legal action, but eventually the matter was allowed to drop.

DAME JUDI DENCH

Dame Judi Dench appeared in *Mrs Brown*, the 1997 movie which earned her first of seven Academy Award nominations. She recalled how much fun she had appearing with Billy Connolly in the film.

Dench revealed that while they were filming at Osborne House, Queen Victoria's holiday home on the Isle of Wight, a 'gassy' horse had made it hard for her to keep in royal character. During one scene she had to mount a horse. She explained, 'I got on to this pony, which I had to do from a pair of library stairs,' as she was clad in an enormously heavy costume. 'But the poor pony, as we walked … the pony farted at every single step we took.

'And Billy said, "Is that you? Is it you?"'

In 2021 Dame Judi and newspaper astrologer Mystic Meg teamed up to own a horse called Amsby. The actress revealed the reason for the name, 'My grandson is called Sam and he always used to spell his name Ams, the wrong way round.'

Dame Judi's 10-1 Smokey Oakey bagged her a cool £77,900 when winning the William Hill Lincoln at Doncaster in March 2008.

She also co-owned the Paul Nicholls-trained As De Mee, who was a fancy for the 2018 Grand National before being pulled out.

DE WALDEN, LORD HOWARD

As a gentleman who once very nearly rid the world of one of its worst dictators and, in a racing context, owned one of the great Champion Hurdlers, Lanzarote – who won it in 1974 but was fatally injured in the 1977 Cheltenham Gold Cup – as well as 1985 Derby winner Slip Anchor, Lord Howard de Walden was almost certainly used to being treated with respect.

And in September 1972 when he was accepting a trophy after the victory of his Pursuit Of Love at Doncaster, it was probably just as well that the 79-year-old was not aware of what viewers of *Channel 4 Racing* were being subjected over the presentation pictures.

'Get out of the way, Lord Howard, you old fart,' was the slightly unexpected phrase being uttered by a disembodied voice as the presentation was shown. As well as TV viewers, racegoers listening to the course's own PA system were also able to hear the less-than-complimentary remark, followed by another as, reportedly, the programme's director Bob Gardam sighed, 'Help the aged!' when Lord Howard accepted the race trophy.

When in Munich, learning the German language in 1931, Lord Howard had been behind the wheel of the car he had just purchased when he managed to knock down a pedestrian who, explained the noble lord, gave his name as 'Adolf Hitler'.

STEVE HARLEY

The pop singer, whose classic song 'Make Me Smile (Come Up and See Me)', gave him a smash hit, declared, 'I've lived a life and I've just lived it all again in two minutes there. This was as exciting as anything for me – and I've done a lot.' Harley was talking about his emotional experience as the race horse Cockney Rebel, whose name was borrowed from Steve to christen the horse of that name, won a racing Classic in 2007 – the 2,000 Guineas.

There was further racing chat as Steve was being interviewed on Derby day in 2018 by Stephen Taylor of Wolverhampton What's On, prior to a concert, 'It's Derby day and, as Steve Harley is preparing to go on stage at the Acoustic Festival of Britain, our conversation is punctuated by racing commentaries from Doncaster and Epsom.

'"I've had one of my biggest bets for five years," says the 67-year-old. "It's a horse that my friends own and they swear it's gonna win. The horse is called Austrian School."

'Harley is a passionate racing fan, so it's fitting that our interview is taking place at Uttoxeter Racecourse.

'With our interview almost at an end, Harley politely asked if he could watch the Derby, having seen his earlier tip fail to make it into the frame.

'"I'm sorry, it's the Derby, and I might just get my losses back."

'As we watched the horses approach the last half mile, the live stream of the race froze, resulting in a volley of expletives from Harley. Later, he announced during a very impressive set, that he'd backed the winner as well as the second-placed horse in the Derby. So all in all a good day at the races for the legendary Cockney Rebel, both on the turf at Epsom and on stage at Uttoxeter.'

In a 2012 *Express* interview, Harley said, 'I travel a lot, play a lot and every time I walk on stage I don't know what is going to happen. Racing feeds that same passion in me. I made friends with a racing journalist, Marten Julian, and he was friends with Mel Smith. In the early 1980s they said they were forming a syndicate and asked would I like to come in. We shared a wonderful grey handicap hurdler, Cloudwalker. He was a lovely horse and won nine times which is considerable. People can own horses all their life and never get a winner.

'I like to say that I am not a gambler but I am a betting man. There is a subtle difference.'

On his website, Steve revealed his unfulfilled ambition: 'I only wish I could have ridden a big, good steeplechaser over the Cheltenham course just once in my life.'

MICHAEL HOLDING

This legendary West Indies cricketer has been a long-term lover of horseracing from his early school days, writing on his website, michael-holding.com , 'It's no secret that I have a long established love affair with horseracing. From the first moment I saw the magnificent thoroughbreds at Caymanas Park in Kingston as a young child, I was fascinated, but playing cricket and football occupied so much of my time and energy that I didn't rekindle my interest properly until I reached the third form at Kingston College.

'Some class-mates seemed to know everything there was to know about the local racing scene, and not wanting to sound ignorant I decided to go out to Caymanas Park on race days to acquaint myself with the whole ambience around the horses, trainers and jockeys. Eventually I got to know just about everything there was to know and earned the nickname "Tempus" around my school-mates. The original Tempus was a horse at Caymanas Park and I had more faith in him than his form actually merited.'

Holding, a long-term friend of trainer Sir Michael Stoute, confessed, 'I am an avid spectator of horseracing, but paradoxically I prefer to watch racing on TV in the comfort of my home rather than trackside as you don't actually see much of the horses there.'

Michael received one of THE great racing accolades when he was given the opportunity to take part in Royal Ascot's royal presentation in 2009, 'I was forewarned that the Queen would be calling me to ask if I would like to attend so [wife] Laurie-Ann and I went to have lunch with Her Majesty at Windsor Castle before joining the procession in the carriages for that famous ride down the Ascot straight, then we spent the rest of the day in the Royal Box. It was a real honour.'

LILLIE LANGTRY

Rock group The Who enjoyed a huge chart hit in 1967 with their song 'Pictures of Lily'. In his 2012 memoir *Who I Am*, the band's songwriter Pete Townshend references Lillie (as Lily) Langtry the music hall star and mistress of Edward VII as his inspiration for the track. Indeed, as mentioned in its lyrics, Lillie died in the year 1929.

Born in 1852 in Jersey to the Rev Corbet le Breton and christened Emilie Charlotte, as a child Lillie was something of a tomboy due to her upbringing with six brothers.

But Lillie was just a teenager when she and her brother Reggie teamed up to pay '30 shillings', or £4 (depending on which account you choose to believe) for a mare named Flirt who they had spotted running down the field in a race at Gorey Common and decided they could improve enough to win a race for them.

In her excellently researched 1973 book *Ladies In Racing*, Caroline Ramsden wrote, 'They stabled her secretly in an outhouse at the deanery, feeding her on whatever they could scrounge from the fodder provided for the rest of the family horses.'

Lillie rode her out in the local lanes while Reginald sharpened her up with gallops and they then entered her for a £30 selling race in which she was ridden to victory by Reggie, thus changing ownership when she was sold on.

'The prophetically named Flirt kindled in Lillie a passion for racing that she maintained into old age,' explained Jersey racing historian John Henwood.

Lillie met and married wealthy Irish widower and large sailing yacht owner Edward Langtry, 26, in 1874 at St Saviour's Church on the island before moving to the mainland, and, tired of being known as Emilie Charlotte, she dumped those names in favour of Lillie – rather than Lily.

Lillie had insisted that she and her new husband should move to London, and in 1876 they rented an apartment in Eaton Place, Belgravia, before moving to Norfolk Street, off Park Lane, to accommodate the by now growing demands of Lillie's society visitors, via whom she was soon sought after by prominent artists.

However, she clearly wasn't the monogamous type. Lillie soon became one of the most celebrated actresses and beauties of her day, owing some of her notoriety to an intimate relationship with the Prince of Wales, later to become King Edward VII.

The future monarch was so enamoured of her charms that they shared a love nest in Bournemouth, which would later become the Langtry Manor Hotel, where late 20th- and 21st-century guests were invited to attend grand dinners in the presence of actors taking the roles of the 'Jersey Lily', as she became popularly known.

Built in 1877 by the Prince of Wales for Lillie, the house is unique in Bournemouth. Designed by Lillie herself and executed in the style of a Victorian country house, it retains to this day many of its original features – balconied bedrooms, carved fireplaces, mullioned windows and elegant staircases.

To discover more of the history of the hotel, the Langtry Collection, set on the first floor, explores the life of Lillie. Many notable figures of the day were also entertained at Langtry Manor, or the Red House as the Prince and Lillie liked to call it.

Lillie's liaison with the Prince lasted for a couple of years. Although they remained friends, the physical relationship ended when Lillie became pregnant, probably by old friend Arthur Jones, who accompanied her to Paris for the birth of the child, Jeanne Marie, in March 1881.

In July 1879, Lillie had begun an affair with the Earl of Shrewsbury, and it is said that the couple were planning to elope together. But in the autumn of that year, scandal-mongering journalist Adolphus Rosenberg wrote of rumours that her long-suffering husband would divorce her and cite, among others, the Prince of Wales as co-respondent, which resulted in the end of that relationship.

To today's contemporary eyes Lillie may not appear to be conventionally glamorous, but by the standards of the late 19th century she was a 'startling beauty', wrote Caroline Ramsden.

From 1882 to 1891, Langtry is said to have had a relationship with US millionaire Frederic Gebhard. In 1885 she and Gebhard brought a stable of American horses to race in England. On 13 August 1888, Langtry and Gebhard travelled in her private car attached to an express train bound for Chicago.

Another railcar was transporting 17 of their horses when it derailed in Pennsylvania at 1.40am. Rolling down an 80ft embankment, it burst into flames. One person died in the fire, along with Gebhard's champion runner Eole and 14 race horses belonging to Langtry and him. One of the two horses to survive the wreck was St Saviour, named after St Saviour's Church in Jersey, where Langtry's father had been rector, and where Lillie ultimately chose to be buried.

Lillie caught the eye of artist John Everett Millais, whose subsequent painting of her holding a nerine lily became very famous and was eventually offered for sale by an anonymous vendor at Sotheby's in March 1973 when it was purchased by John Appleby for 9,500gns, later becoming the property of the States of Jersey.

Friends of Lillie encouraged her to act, and, aged 29 when she began, she duly wowed the public in this guise and maintained her theatrical career for 30 years at home and abroad.

Lillie enjoyed attending big race meetings of the day and although she hadn't owned a race horse since Flirt, in 1892 she was gifted ownership of a two-year-old named Milford, whether by Prince Batthyany or, more likely, the Squire Abington Baird, remains somewhat unclear.

However, the horse was extremely useful and won Ascot's Coventry Stakes and Newmarket's July Stakes although failing to train on as a three-year-old. Lillie won £8,000 in prize money through Milford, who she had trained at Sam Pickering's stables near Newmarket.

She was encouraged to buy more horseflesh for Pickering to oversee, as well as a house, Regal Lodge, close to the stables. Nobleman proved to be a winner for her, while Lady Roseberry won the Lanark Cup and the Jockey Club Cup as even-money favourite over two and a quarter miles, both in 1893, and was also second in the Cesarewitch – one of the calendar's longest flat races, for which Lillie became a great enthusiast and became determined to win.

Lillie soon had some 20 horses running in her colours, which she registered with Weatherbys as turquoise and fawn hoops with turquoise cap – as these happened to be the colours she was wearing when the decision had to be made. Back then ladies weren't officially permitted to admit to being owners, so she had to adopt the pseudonym 'Mr Jersey' on race cards carrying the names of her runners.

A friend of Lillie's, racing journalist William Allison, arranged for her to purchase, for a reported 1,600gns, a promising Australian horse who had won a decent race called the Williamstown Cup.

The horse was Merman, who was duly shipped over and 'acclimatised' in low-profile races and then, trained by William 'Jack' Robinson, entered for a handicap at Lewes which he won under a jockey named Sharples, with a hefty Lillie wager on his back before romping home in Newmarket's 13 October 1897 Cesarewitch at odds of 100-7 under jockey Fred Webb, landing Lillie a reported £39,000 in winning bets.

Lillie's friend, the Prince of Wales, also enjoyed a wager and was also 'on' Merman, to the extent that he gave the jockey a royal seal of approval, having him brought to see and shake hands with him.

However, the elation of victory reportedly turned into despair for Lillie as her by-now estranged, and quite possibly ex-husband, committed suicide shortly after the event. During her own travels in the United States, Lillie had become an American citizen, and reportedly, on 13 May 1897, divorced husband Edward in California. He clearly didn't take it well.

Chester Lunatic Asylum reported the death of Edward on 17 October 1897, four days after the Cesarewitch, a newspaper story explaining that he had been arrested two days earlier at Crewe Railway Station 'where he was found wandering in a demented condition' having just arrived back in the country from America.

Respected racing writer Tony Morris wrote in 2012, 'Papers carried the contrasting stories of Lillie's great success and her husband's pathetic demise. The wholly positive publicity she had expected to enjoy inevitably failed to materialise. Over the next few days she was having to make statements to the effect that she had regularly made Ned an adequate allowance since their separation, and even to deny that she had arranged his murder.'

After her divorce, Lillie had been linked to Prince Louis Esterhazy – both had an interest in horseracing.

Lillie won the 1897 Liverpool Cup with Brayhead, the 1898 Lewes Handicap and 1899 Prince Edward Cup with Maluma, while in the latter year the Lewes Handicap went to her Uniform.

On 23 July 1899, Merman had started as the 4-1 favourite in the Liverpool Cup at Manchester, and finished fifth. Three days later Merman ran at the Glorious Goodwood meeting in the 2m Goodwood Plate and as the 4-1 second-favourite won the event easily by four lengths.

On 27 July Lillie married 28-year-old Hugo Gerald de Bathe at St Saviour's Church and was also, say some reports, present to witness her horse capture the prestigious Goodwood Cup over the 2.5m distance at 6-5 second-favourite.

The horse also went on to win the Ascot Gold Cup, surviving rumours that 'the cup might be taken from him on a technicality', wrote Dorothy Laird in her 1976 book *Royal Ascot*, in which she added that although the horse was then scheduled to start later in the week for the Alexandra Plate, 'Mrs Langtry sent orders that he was not to run ... and his absence from the post after being seen in the paddock seemed to give colour to the report that there was an objection against him for the cup on the grounds of some informality in the nomination.'

Despite both jockey Sloan and trainer Robinson urging Lillie to keep Merman in training, she opted to send him to stud, where, however, he never sired a horse of any consequence. In 2016 Merman was inducted to the Australian Racing Hall of Fame.

Lillie had met 'The Squire' – a 'rake' of the day – at Newmarket races in April 1891 when he insisted that she change her intended bet to place her money on his horse, Quartus, instead. Quartus promptly won at odds of 5-2. He then handed her a roll of cash and told her to back his runner, Macunas, in a later race – which also won. Having accepted his invitation to dine together, she was soon infatuated, and they became lovers.

He honoured her by a somewhat different 'sporting' event – the staging of a 'rat-pit' in the foyer of London's Haymarket Theatre, at which the friends of her beau, the Squire, were 'invited to try their dogs against cagefuls of London sewage rats'.

Lillie was not best pleased when womaniser Baird, born in 1861, and who had won the Derby with the appropriately named Merry Hampton, decamped to America with several of his cronies in 1893, only to die there on 18 March that same year.

She was reportedly somewhat more distressed by the revelation that she did not figure in his will, rather than by his somewhat earlier than expected demise. A Scottish newspaper reported that much of his fortune had been 'squandered on horse-racing, prize-fighting and harlotry'. The remainder, such as it was, went to his mother and family, at which news, it was reported, Lille became 'greatly distressed'.

Sporting Life had reported on 22 March in 'a despatch from Nice', 'Mrs Langtry heard of the death of Mr Baird while cruising in the Mediterranean on the Whyte Ladye. She made for this port with all haste, and displayed great anxiety to return to England immediately.'

Baird, who was also said to have been violent towards her on occasion, had apparently gifted her the yacht.

In 1900 Merman was entered for one of the sport's greatest events, the Royal Ascot Gold Cup, where the horse would be ridden by American jockey Tod Sloan, who had popularised the favoured riding style of US jockeys of pulling up their knees and crouching over their horse's neck, which seemed to distribute their weight more evenly during races. Lillie and her trainer, Robinson, feared the horse wasn't fit enough, but Sloan convinced them to take their chance, and the 20-1 long-odds outsider duly won, leaving the jockey bemoaning that fact that he was paid only 'the usual five-guinea fee' and adding bitterly, 'And the stewards blame jockeys for betting!'

Perhaps her big-time racing swansong was Yentoi who, in 1908 at 100-6, won one of the longest races in the calendar, the Cesarewitch, a favourite race for Lillie, trained by Fred Darling and ridden by Freddie Fox.

When the First World War broke out, Lillie was appearing in a play in the US. She returned to Regal Lodge in 1917 but once the conflict was over she sold her racing interests and properties and moved to Monaco.

Lillie was years ahead of her time by using her celebrity to earn large amounts of money by endorsing commercial products such as cosmetics and soap.

Lillie died aged 75 on 12 February 1929 in Monte Carlo, before being returned to be buried in Jersey. She had asked to be buried in her parents' tomb at St Saviour's Church. Due to blizzards, transport was delayed. Her body was taken to St Malo and across to Jersey on 22 February aboard a steamer. Her coffin lay in St Saviour's overnight surrounded by flowers, and she was buried on the afternoon of 23 February.

Her beauty continued to make an impression long after her death. In 1978, her story was dramatised on television in *Lillie*, starring Francesca Annis.

But perhaps her ultimate accolade happened in 1994 when, in an episode of *The Simpsons*, entitled 'Burns Heir', Mr Burns is depicted as owning, on his estate, the 'Lillie Langtry Theater'.

The memory of one of the most glamorous and scandalous women of the late 19th and early 20th century was again commemorated on Saturday, 1 August 2020 at the first race meeting with spectators to be held at an English racecourse since the previous March, when the final day of the annual Glorious Goodwood festival featured the Lillie Langtry Stakes.

ADAM LINDSAY GORDON

Adam Lindsay Gordon was a British-Australian poet, horseman, police officer and politician, and the first Aussie poet to gain significant recognition overseas.

As well as this talent, he had another for riding horses, and set a record by becoming the only jockey to have ridden three winners over jumps in one day, at Flemington in 1868. Already a leading amateur rider despite being short-sighted, he jumped up on Babbler who, despite carrying a hefty 13st 4lb, was the 3-1 favourite for the Hunt Club Cup and despite needing two attempts to clear one fence, horse and poet won.

He then climbed on to his own horse, Viking, 5-2 favourite in the five-runner race, to contest the 3m Metropolitan Handicap Steeplechase, gaining a straightforward win.

His possible hat-trick horse was Cadger in the Selling Steeplechase, who turned out to be the easiest of his three victories, against just two rivals.

Sadly the troubled writer took his own life in June 1870, aged just 36. The Adam Lindsay Gordon monument was erected in 1950 between Coleraine and Casterton, remembering, 'The great Australian poet who rode in the Great Western Steeplechase, distance about four miles, and crossed the road at this point, first run in 1858. The great sportsman was a contestant in this famous event for five years, 1862–66. Concerning the race he wrote, "On the fields of Coleraine there'll be labor in vain. Before the Great Western is ended the nags will have toiled and the silks will have soiled. And the rails will require to be mended."'

SIR ANDREW LLOYD WEBBER

Reflecting on the Lloyd Webber-owned Black Humour's fourth place in the 1993 Hennessy, trainer Charlie Brooks revealed, 'I sat on the kitchen floor and hit my head against the fridge door all night.'

During the same year, Sir Andrew's wife Madeleine's Al Mutahm, potentially a Champion Hurdle prospect, bought for her for a reported £80,000 by her husband, tragically suffered a fatal accident during a hurdles race at Newbury.

In 1994 Sir Andrew bought Madeleine a five per cent share in Newbury racecourse for a reported £200,000.

In June 2014 a big win was music to the ears of Sir Andrew, as his runner The Fugue sprang an 11-2 surprise in the Group 1

Prince of Wales's Stakes at Royal Ascot, worth £297,727.50, and leaving the previous year's horse of the year, the French filly Treve, trailing in her wake.

The Fugue coasted home in a new track record under William Buick, causing the owner to gush, 'It's the best day of our racing career.'

The five-year-old mare had one more race before quitting the track, with earnings of £1.9m to her credit, and having won six of her 19 races.

In October 2021, the Lloyd Webbers collected a seven-figure payout after a horse he bred was sold. Sir Andrew had arrived at Newmarket just in time to see the bidding hit £600,000 for a horse being sold from his Watership Down stud.

But the asking price continued to increase for the yearling by legendary race horse Sea The Stars, and the hammer eventually went down for £1.2m.

Sir Andrew said, 'I got here just in time in a taxi, I just walked in at the 600,000 mark.'

Watership Down Stud was founded by Andrew and Madeleine in 1992. With the aid of racing manager Simon Marsh, they renovated the old stable yards so that they were suitable for foaling mares and set about fencing thousands of acres of grassland. Much of the land had only been grazed by sheep and boasted some of the finest grassland in the UK.

Since the stud's completion, their policy has been to buy and develop top-class bloodlines, often selling the colts and keeping the fillies which they breed.

Their first major broodmare purchase was Silver Lane for $750,000 in 1993. She was carrying Black Hawk, who won over £3.5m in prize money and later produced Shakespeare, who was sold as a yearling for 2.2m guineas.

A year later, Watership Down purchased Darara, a Group 1-winning daughter of Darshaan. She went on to become one of the world's all-time best broodmares, producing four Group 1 winners including Dar Re Mi, who carried the Lloyd Webbers' colours to Group 1 glory on three occasions. Darara also bred a colt by Sadler's Wells who sold for 3.4million guineas as a yearling in 2000.

Kiltinan Castle Stud was purchased by the Lloyd Webbers in 1996. Andrew was struck by the beauty of the castle and its stunning grounds with the River Clashawley flowing down from Slievenamon, one of Ireland's most unspoilt mountains.

Madeleine was already sending mares to stallions at Coolmore Stud, which is adjacent to Kiltinan, and the decision was taken to develop Kiltinan into a stud farm.

Thanks to its rich pasture, Kiltinan is perfect for nurturing young stock and provides the perfect location for mares visiting Coolmore as well as other leading stud farms in Ireland.

Watership Down Stud-owned mares had produced 186 foals by mid-2022, who between them had won over £20m in prize money.

In 2009 Dar Re Mi won the Audi Pretty Polly Stakes at the Curragh, after which Madeleine joked with Audi boss John Hayes, 'We'll send you a CD, if you send us an Audi.'

PAUL McCARTNEY

Sir Paul McCartney has had a love for animals from an early age, and in 1964 the Beatle splashed out £1,200 to buy a race horse named Drake's Drum for his father Jim, which he gave him as a 62nd birthday present.

Paul told Jim about his four legged-gift on the evening of the *A Hard Day's Night* premiere. Paul said, 'My father likes a flutter – he is one of the world's greatest armchair punters.'

In 1966 Paul almost overshadowed even the Grand National as his dad's horse won the 6f Hutton Plate at Aintree – the race immediately before the main event – and Macca led the horse in after the race then watched 50-1 shot Anglo win the National. Drake's Drum won four times during 1966.

In 2015, Sir Paul had a unique rocking horse commissioned to be auctioned to raise money for Alder Hey, the children's hospital in Liverpool.

'All You Horse Riders' is a song written and performed by McCartney, recorded during sessions for his *McCartney II* album in 1979. It remained officially unissued until the re-issue edition in 2011, part of his archive collection.

JOHN McCRIRICK

Lee Mottershead of the *Racing Post* captured the appeal of John McCririck with the comment: '"Big Mac" was one of very few characters who ever "broke out" of the horseracing bubble to achieve wider recognition with the great British public, and even farther afield.'

Lee was spot on – only Frankie Dettori, of his contemporaries, could match Mac's recognition factor. He even appeared on the prestigious BBC TV current affairs debate programme *Question Time*, and in mass entertainment shows such as *Celebrity Big Brother*.

Declared jockey turned writer Marcus Armytage when news broke of John's death on 15 July 2019 at the age of 79, 'In a world increasingly devoid of such creatures, McCririck was an eccentric and huge character. There is no way of measuring it, but I dare say he drew more people to the sport than anyone else. He was unique, a one-off, and most of us will miss him.'

Yet behind the grandstanding, blustering big mouth hid an award-winning investigative journalist, a fearless TV interviewer who would challenge influential racing figures, usually indulged and soft-soaped by his contemporaries.

He was also a man who, despite giving the impression that he didn't give a damn what the public thought of him, clearly did – as racing writer Simon Nott discovered when, with John very close to death, he was asked by the pundit's wife Jenny to prepare an obituary which she could distribute to the media.

Nott wrote, 'Jenny knew John was going to die very soon, and asked me whether I could write a short obituary for her to use. Of course I was going to accede to the request, and spent some time preparing it before sending it off to her.

'It wasn't long before Jenny contacted me again to tell me John was working on proof-reading and amending the obituary I had supplied, even down to adding an apostrophe! How many people ever get – or would even want – to correct their own obituary?'

McCririck began his career at the *Sporting Life*, where he twice won at the British Press Awards for his campaigning journalism, but he was sacked in 1984. In 1981 he joined ITV Sport's horseracing coverage, which became, during 1984 and 1985, *Channel 4 Racing*.

From the 1980s onwards he made numerous appearances on British television, including as a contestant on *The Weakest Link*, *Wife Swap* and *After Dark*.

An only child, he was born in Surbiton before his family moved to the Channel island of Jersey, to St Helier where they lived in a house 'that was later the HQ of Jersey television' whose grounds apparently included a 2,000-pear tree orchard. His father ran a property business.

John was sent off to boarding school, and completed his schooling at Harrow – as did Winston Churchill, albeit not at the same time. There he met Julian Wilson, who would go on to become the BBC's main television racing presenter and editor. John also entered the bookmaking world at Harrow where he ran a book on school cross country races. His 'scruffy appearance led to beatings', reported his *Times* obituary. McCririck claimed he was Wilson's 'fag'.

Leaving school with three O-levels to his name, he failed to pass an interview for the diplomatic service and instead took a job as a waiter at the world-famous Dorchester Hotel – a career which ceased after he spilled soup over a guest.

Now he found his way to the racecourse as a bookie's runner, while living in 'squalid bedsits', setting up briefly as a racecourse bookie himself. He also worked in betting shops. On the racecourse he became fluent in the bookies' private sign language, tic-tac. Likewise his colourful racing and betting slang language usage helped his image – waving his arms he would yell 'Burlington Bertie, 100 to 30' or 'top of the head, nine to four' as he reported the latest odds.

Via Wilson, John got a job as a results sub-editor on the BBC TV sports programme *Grandstand*. He also began to make a name for himself as a racing journalist and in 1978 had been named Specialist Writer of the Year at the British Press Awards for uncovering scandals associated with greyhound racing.

A year later he was the Campaigning Journalist of the Year for exposing corruption at The Tote. In 1981 he began working for ITV – the year Shergar won the Derby.

He was fired from *Sporting Life* in 1984, but in the same year began working for Channel 4's racing team. He also sued the *Daily Star* over a story 'involving his relationship with a bookmaker', winning damages as a result.

John was prone to 'dissing' himself in interviews, presenting himself as a grudge-bearer and sexist. 'Part of his act was a casual sexism,' noted his *Times* obituary. 'Those who haven't got big chests have no chance with me,' he once declared.

'How much this was true and how much a deliberate inflation to outrage the press was never completely clear,' said *The Times*.

During your author's lengthy acquaintanceship with John during my time as a spokesman for bookies William Hill, I never found him anything but straightforward, friendly, humorous and helpful.

Jenny herself said his sexism was a 'façade' in a *Daily Mail* interview, adding, 'John's not like that in real life. He's actually very generous, kind and extremely hard-working.'

They met at a party and were married in 1970 at Marylebone Register Office. He once declared, 'Without Jenny to handle things my life would be a shambles.'

Every midnight she would be sent to King's Cross to buy the next day's papers for him to study and prepare for his next broadcasts. He would later sleep briefly, being woken at around 6am with a glass of chilled orange juice as his bath was being run for him.

Guardian journalist Stephen Moss reported, 'He can't drive so she ferries him to race meetings. Nor can he cook, mend a fuse, or do anything else practical, so she has to attend to the business of living. He does a review of the papers on Channel 4's *Morning Line* at 9am each Saturday, and you can guess who is down at King's Cross station at midnight buying the papers. They have no children; or perhaps they have one extremely large child.

'If he wasn't a TV star, he would be a pitiable figure; indeed a potential supplicant. He can afford to celebrate his multiple failures because when it comes to synchronised arm-waving and on-camera histrionics he is sensational.'

Mac had strong opinions on many aspects of racing, in July 2001 giving Moss his opinion on use of the whip in racing, 'The only living things you can hit are horses, and it just cannot be right. It's the unacceptable side of racing. They use euphemisms – "giving them a reminder", "waking him up", and all that sort of thing. The best horses would still win. One or two results would be different, but so what? Horses can't tell you if they are in pain.'

Not notably left-wing, McCririck also gave Moss the benefit of his opinions of some of the unemployed, 'There are millions of people begging the rest of us to help them. If you're very old or you're sick, fine, but there are millions of people who are capable of working who are still coming to us for money. There are people who are taking money, my money, and going into betting shops and betting on horses [his voice rises several octaves at this point]. That's not what the welfare state was set up for. It was meant to be a failsafe system to stop people falling through the net. Now it's a hammock.'

John made a spectacle of himself yet again in 1996 – literally so, as he won the Spectacle Wearer of the Year award, at least thus proving his instant recognisability.

That year also saw demands being made for John to be removed from the nation's TV screens, with Warwick Bartlett, chairman of the British Betting Offices Association, declaring in February, 'We'll be asking the chief executive of Channel 4 to have Mr McCririck removed, as we consider him to be past his sell-by date. We are also asking our members to write to all female MPs to draw their attention to the fact that McCririck is chauvinistic towards women, who represent about 25 per cent of our customer base.'

Mac responded bullishly, 'If Warwick Bartlett wishes to draw up a petition to get me sacked by *C4 Racing*, then he will be swamped by people eager to add their signatures. I have to agree that Warwick Bartlett has caught the public mood and is on to a sure-fire winner.' Of course, John well knew that Warwick had done no such thing.

During the same year, on Grand National day, John was quoted by the *Daily Sport* – and I do not believe he denied making the comment – as suggesting 'a Page 3 National', explaining, 'We could have Page 3 girls jumping over fences topless – and I could be one of the fences.'

By 2006, John was not only known throughout the UK, but his fame had spread abroad – even if the Americans weren't quite sure why. A full-page colour photo of him featured in a book listing all American racecourses with the caption, 'John McCririck, famed British bookmaker.'

Declared the authors of the book *Horse Racing: The Traveler's Guide to the Sport of Kings*, in a section devoted to the Breeders' Cup, 'British racing personality and bookie, John "Muttonchops" McCrirrick [sic] is always on hand – sometimes wrapped snugly inside a buffalo robe and Davy Crockett cap, other times suitably duded-out in western boots, suede jacket, bolo and, uh, a good-guy-white straw hat. While hand signalling his picks to the bookmakers back home, he's glad to toss betting tips to the tens of thousands of spectators assembled at the racetrack.'

John's claim that his not entirely mutually agreed departure from the Channel 4 team was due to age discrimination was lost during 2013. He observed, 'After such a landmark judicial verdict, my failed legal action ensures that anonymous suits and skirts, who control the media, numerous other businesses and the public sector, will now enjoy complete freedom to replace older employees whatever their unimpaired ability and merit.

'I have let them all down along with my wife … my legal team, friends, colleagues and countless members of the public who supported me throughout. My grateful thanks and apologies to every one of them. Former Labour home secretary David Blunkett MP said in August, "The way TV executives worship the cult of youth seems to be an unstoppable fetish." It is now.'

The employment tribunal, however, accepted that McCririck was dismissed 'because of his persona emanating from his appearances from celebrity television shows ... His style of dress, attitudes, opinions and tic-tac gestures were not in keeping with the new aims and his opinions seen as arrogant and confrontational'.

Following John's death, *Times* columnist Carol Midgley recalled visiting their home when she went to interview Jenny, aka 'the Booby', a name which, John explained, came from a South American bird which, like her, was 'stupid, squawks a lot and is easy to catch.'

Midgley reported, 'He never gave her birthday cards or presents, never once did the washing up, literally couldn't turn on the oven. He once rang her while she was out riding to say, "I can't get the kettle to work." He had switched it on at the plug but not pushed the button down. He was 64.'

However, contemplating the fact that the two had been married for 48 years at the time, Midgley pointed out, 'It seemed perfectly clear to me that Jenny liked the marriage the way it was, her mothering him. It obviously worked for them.'

John appeared in *Celebrity Big Brother*, dubbing 'supermodel' and fellow housemate Caprice 'the totty', and after the programme finished he was voted as the second-most hated man in Britain – after Simon Cowell. John would now pop up on satellite TV channel At The Races rather than the main networks. An unlikely tabloid rumour suggested he was being considered for the role of the next Dr Who and conjured up 'death threats from members of the Doctor Who Appreciation Society'.

In April 2016 John made the tabloids when he accused *Fifty Shades of Grey* movie director Sam Taylor-Johnson and her actor husband Aaron of being 'neighbours from hell' by renting out their house to people who then threw 'raves' at their £14m home in London's Primrose Hill, located behind the McCrٳricks' mews house, valued at the time at £1.4m by the *Daily Mail*.

Ranted John to *Mail* showbusiness correspondent Tim Lamden, 'The noise can be absolutely terrible. It's so selfish and inconsiderate, but what can you do?' in an outburst which some might have thought to reflect the way his own TV performances were often criticised.

Added Mac, 'You might get attacked or slagged off if you go round and tell them to be quiet. I've lost sleep because of the banging and music that's been going on. It's really terrible.'

John appeared in several TV shows, including *Celebrity Wife Swap* – in which he swapped partners with former MP Edwina Currie and her husband. Edwina called him 'rude' and 'crude' and at one point threw champagne over him. It is difficult to know how much of this might have been staged or suggested in the interests of controversial viewing.

He and Jenny never had children, but kept cats called Lost and Found, and a Labrador named Smelly.

'His impact on the popularity of racing should not be underestimated,' said *Times* racing editor Rob Wright. 'He was one of those rare people involved in the sport able to make an impression on the wider public.'

One of the few racing figures better known than Big Mac, Frankie Dettori, said after John's death, 'I met him for the first time when I was 16 and an apprentice. I always got on really well with him. He was very flamboyant and controversial. He did put on a bit of a show but underneath it all he worked very hard and was very knowledgeable.'

When Big Mac died some racecourses were quick to pay tribute to him – such as Sandown, where on 6 July 2019, for Eclipse Stakes day, the programme contained a full page, featuring a large photo of John, and told readers, 'Outlandish, but enormously respected within the racing and bookmaking industries, he will be missed by all who had the pleasure of meeting or working with him.'

When *Racing Post*'s Peter Thomas went to interview John in June 2014 he found, 'Memorabilia adorns every spare inch of space – and a few more inches that aren't spare – in the living room.'

That included photos of John with Margaret Thatcher, and Prince Khalid Abdullah, and 'countless portraits' of him that 'either flatter or condemn, depending on your point of view'.

Mac justified this – 'It's a shrine to me.'

After seeing John demanding and the Booby providing, Thomas pondered, 'To the casual observer their relationship – his whole life for that matter – is like the light in a refrigerator; you want to know what happens to it when you close the door and walk away.'

As John's notoriety or celebrity began to fade, Thomas, who saw him sitting watching *The Jeremy Kyle Show*, rather than appearing on it, felt that the man 'who once threw darts underarm with Phil "The Power" Taylor, went *Through the Keyhole*, upstaged Richard and Judy, Anne and Nick and Dick and Dom, and succumbed to the advances of *Loose Women* is now the reluctant viewer, rather than the grateful object of televisual ire and indignation'.

Returning from Cheltenham's 2009 New Year's Day meeting, the Macs were shocked to discover they had been burgled and their home ransacked.

Standing, stunned, among the mess, John answered the phone – and found himself talking to a man who was claiming to have carried out the burglary.

'I was very calm,' said John, 'and found myself saying things like, "How many bottles of champagne did you take?"'

The burglar said he had been looking for shotguns – but John denied owning one.

'I told him the jewellery he took wasn't worth anything but that it was of great sentimental value to my wife. He said he would give it back and would call again to tell me where he would leave it. He didn't.'

Despite taking televisions, several hundred pounds in cash and gold shirt studs, the offender didn't take any of John's awards.

Later in May of the same year, Channel 4 racing presenter Alice Plunkett told *Racing Post* of a disturbing scene she had witnessed, 'John McCririck calling "Mummy, Mummy, Mummy" with his head in his hands when things got a little fraught a couple of seasons ago – very worrying!'

After John died, Jenny put some of his iconic items up for auction in December 2019, raising around £30,000 in the process. The highest-profile item was John's familiar gold and diamond horseshoe-shaped ring which went for £5,500 and, said Rowley's auction house's Roddy Lloyd, 'encapsulated him, as he always had a ring on every finger'.

Jenny said part of the reason for the sale was that she was worried thieves would target her because of the jewellery that her husband was famous for wearing. Among the other items offered were a collection of cigars, clothes, some distinctive headwear, footwear, plus jackets and suits – most handmade for the pundit.

Added Jenny, 'I only decided to sell the items because a friend asked me to go to a charity valuation day with her.

'I took some of John's rings – he'd always said that if anything should happen to him I should get them valued.

'John told people they were rubbish because he didn't want them stolen. People would shake his hands and try and take them – that's why his rings were joined together with a chain.

'I was surprised to hear how much they were worth and I was worried about having them stolen – we suffered a burglary some years ago and it was awful.

'I decided to put the rings and some other items in for auction and I also donated some to Cancer Research. Other items have been donated to Palace House, and the National Horseracing Museum in Newmarket, being exhibited there.

'One of the reasons John dressed as he did was to enable his cameraman high in the stands to pick him out at the trackside in the crowd.

'He had his clothes made; he was a big man and it was hard to find off-the-shelf clothes. He also enjoyed cigars and would often get the sound man to hold it while he did his piece to camera.

'John was a showman, it was a panto act; a business. Importantly, the punters knew he cared. If he thought there was something wrong in the racing world he would say so; he would always tell the truth.

'John was a multi-award winning journalist as well as a TV personality.'

Rowley's Lloyd said, 'John McCririck was very much a larger-than-life character – he was also physically big so the clothes are huge.

'John transcended the world of racing and his flamboyant style and distinctive look endeared him to millions.'

There was some doubt about John's date of birth – different sources suggested 15 April or 17 April and he never listed his date of birth in the annual publication *Directory of the Turf.*

John himself claimed never to celebrate his birthday. 'Why should I celebrate the obscenity of getting old?' he asked rhetorically, confirming that he had no interest in birthday parties, either, 'I am not a pleasant man. I have very few friends, if any. I don't go to parties.'

'In a world increasingly devoid of such creatures, McCririck was an eccentric and huge character. There is no way of measuring it, but I dare say he drew more people to the sport than anyone else. He was unique, a one-off, and most of us will miss him,' wrote Marcus Armytage on Twitter.

The late foreign secretary Robin Cook, a fellow racing fan and firm friend, once said of John, 'We were in the garden of his London flat, and he'd bought some outdoor gas heaters that he wanted me, as foreign secretary, to formally turn on. The moment

I went to have the "turning on ceremony", thunder and lightning broke out and we had to run inside.'

The Scotsman reported on 12 August 2005, 'Racing pundit John McCririck today stunned Robin Cook's funeral by launching a blistering attack on Tony Blair's failure to attend the service at Edinburgh's St Giles' Cathedral.

'Speaking in front of most of Britain's leading Labour politicians, Mr Cook's good friend accused the prime minister of "petty vindictiveness".

'He contrasted the decision to remain on a family holiday in the Caribbean with former premiere Margaret Thatcher's attendance at her old rival Ted Heath's funeral earlier this year.

'Mr McCririck told more than 700 mourners, including chancellor Gordon Brown, foreign secretary Jack Straw and most of Mr Blair's cabinet, that Mr Blair had snubbed Mr Cook's widow Gaynor and the rest of the family by staying on holiday.

'He said, "What an impressive attendance we've all got. All of us have changed our plans to show our respect and affection for Robin and for Gaynor and the boys and the family.

'"But there is just one exception to that – and that's the nation's leader, the prime minister. Now Margaret Thatcher, of course, she attended Ted Heath's service. I believe the prime minister's snub to Robin's family, to millions of New Labour voters, demonstrates a petty vindictiveness and a moral failure, opting to continue snorkelling instead of doing his duty. What a contrast with Lady Thatcher."

'The racing pundit said that, even though Margaret Thatcher was not a fan of the late prime minister Ted Heath, she had still attended his funeral.

'Mr McCririck's comments were met with a loud cheer by hundreds of members of the public who had lined the Royal Mile to hear a relay of the service on loudspeakers.

'Mr Cook's widow heard the savage criticism as she sat flanked by his sons Peter and Christopher.'

The *Financial Times* wrote, 'His [John's] comments appeared to unsettle some in the cathedral, including John Prescott, deputy prime minister, and John Reid, defence secretary. Peter Hain, Northern Ireland secretary, said later the remarks were "totally uncalled for".'

Typical Big Mac. People may have loved or loathed him, but no one could deny his sincerity and loyalty to the things, the principles and the people he believed in.

JAMES NESBITT

His love of racing proved him to have the luck of the Irish as his Riverside Theatre, 7-2 favourite ridden by jockey Barry Geraghty and trained by Nicky Henderson, won the Ryanair Chase, worth £148,070 to the winner, at the 2012 Cheltenham Festival.

Nesbitt was quoted as saying, 'Forget the Oscars, I've done it all now. I'm rarely lost for words but I'm very emotional now. It's pasted into the album of my memory. I'll die a happy man.

'It was a glorious celebration of everything that's good about sport, not just horseracing the courage of the horse, the ride of Barry Geraghty.

'The horse was beaten at the last and then Barry asked him for a bit more. He was brave and he was strong. We knew he would stay and we knew he would jump but to have had that brilliant battle, I cannot believe it. It's incredible.'

The horse landed another decent prize for the thespian in December 2013, in the Peterborough Chase, worth £34,170 to the winner, for which he went off as 9-4 favourite.

LESTER PIGGOTT

Probably the greatest-ever British jockey, Lester 'the Long Fellow' Piggott was born on 5 November 1935 and died aged 86.

The most taciturn of men, he rarely seemed to care what people thought of him – perhaps because the majority of those involved in, and who were followers of, racing, openly or secretly admired him.

It was inevitable that Lester would become a jockey, just like father Keith, while his mother Iris Rickaby twice won the Newmarket Town Plate. His uncle, Fred Rickaby, rode three Classic winners, grandfather Ernest Piggott won three Grand Nationals; great grandfather Tom Cannon won the Derby, great grandfather John Barham Day rode 16 Classic winners, and trained seven.

As racing commentator Julian Wilson observed, 'Lester Keith Piggott was born and bred to ride; there was no alternative. His pedigree is the human equivalent to that of the finest thoroughbred.'

Here we compile a few of the stories about Lester which weren't included in the copious tributes to him when news of his death broke on 29 May 2022.

* Asked in 1992 for his opinion of female jockeys, Lester offered, 'Their bottoms are the wrong shape.'

* BRYN CROSSLEY, a fellow rider, described in 1993 his feelings about Lester, 'One of the grandest sights in racing has always been to see Lester hauled before the stewards. He goes in there like Clint Eastwood and he comes out like Clint Eastwood. Lester doesn't give a monkey's.'

* COMING BACK to the saddle after retiring surprised many and in the *1991 Ruff's Guide to the Turf*, noted owner Lord Howard de Walden exclaimed, 'I think Lester's potty. What on earth does he think he's doing? It's all very strange.' Asked at the time how he would find racing on his comeback, Lester told an interviewer, 'It's still the same. One leg each side.'

* FRANKIE DETTORI once told Lester he was so old 'they were going to stuff him and put him in a museum'. But Lester took revenge during a race when, revealed the Italian, 'I felt this hand reach over, and he squeezed me by the balls. He just said, "That will teach you not to be so cheeky."' When the news of Lester's death was announced, Frankie tweeted, 'The greatest of all time. My hero. Rest in peace my friend.'

* GIVING CREDIT TO ANOTHER, Lester attended the funeral of another riding great, 11-time champion jockey Charlie Smirke, describing him as 'certainly the best jockey I've ever seen'.

* SIR HENRY CECIL discussed Lester during an interview with Matt Chapman, telling him, 'He's a fascinating person. Takes quite a lot of getting to know … a very kind person, very good with children. Great sense of humour, too.' But he then added, 'If he'd think he should have won a race and he didn't, he'd get off and you wouldn't see him for dust.'

* DAVID ASHFORTH of the *Racing Post* called Lester 'a genius in a saddle, lost out of one'.

* IRISH DERBY Day in 1977 saw Lester take a tumble pre-race and be told by the course doctor he should stand down from the rest of his rides. His response was , 'Don't be be f***ing silly. I've got to go out there and earn my £14 fee in the next race.'

* JACK JARVIS, a successful trainer, said during the 1950s, 'My biggest failure as a trainer – I never made a gentleman of Lester Piggott.'

* JAILED at one point for tax offences and stripped of his OBE, in 2004 on Derby Day, 'Lester Piggott appeared in the Queen's

role as guest of honour, thereby notching up an unlikely double, having gone on from spending time in one of her jails to acting as her stand-in,' pointed out journalist Will Buckley.

* JOHN BERRY, the Newmarket trainer, wrote, 'The fact that the passing of Lester Piggott at the age of 86 in hospital in Switzerland was the first item on the hourly news bulletins on BBC Radio 4 on Sunday morning tells us all that we need to know: Lester was not merely a national sporting icon or international racing hero, but a figure of worldwide significance whose place in the hearts and minds of the public went far beyond the narrow confines of the sport which he dominated for decades.'

* SIR MARK PRESCOTT recalled a different kind of race – this one on the road – which Piggott just needed to win, 'I went down the hill into Royston and Piggott was right behind me. There was a shortcut in those days at a pub called The Blackbirds and I hurtled into it and you had to turn right, but lo and behold there's Piggott going the wrong way around the roundabout to get in front! No wonder he was champion jockey.'

* MICK EASTERBY claimed to be one of the few trainers to get away without giving Lester a present for riding a winner for him, describing how Piggott rode Valarion to win for him at Pontefract, after which, when Mick pleaded poverty, Lester responded, 'Can't you manage a bag of spuds?'

* NIJINSKY was given the accolade 'the most brilliant horse I've ever ridden' by Lester in 1980. But in 2004 he decided, 'The performance of Sir Ivor was more exhilarating than Nijinsky's. so I have to rank him my best Derby winner.'

* NOT everyone was a Lester fan, and a *Daily Telegraph* review of his 1996 autobiography declared, 'Piggott may be the greatest jockey of his generation, but he is also the greatest bore … a work of monumental tedium … but then what can you expect of a man who calls his cat Tiddles.'

* OTHER jockeys could be frustrated by Lester's 'win at all costs' tactics, causing contemporary rival Scobie Breasley to remember in 1993 that he once told him after a rough Newbury race, 'Lester, if you do that to me again, I'll put my foot so far up your backside it will take me a week to get it out.'

* LESTER was also notorious for 'jocking off' his rivals, but was unrepentant, 'It is part of a jockey's job to get on the best horses, and if that involves ruffling a few feathers, so be it.'

* SIR PETER O'SULLEVAN once said that Piggott's attitude resembled 'the gunfighter's delusion of being above the law'.

* ROBERT ELLIS, an owner for whom Lester rode Pirate Way to win at 100-8 at Nottingham, recalled giving him a 'most attractive Brazilian stone set of ashtrays' as a gift, to which Lester responded, 'I'd rather have a cheque.' On another occasion, at Doomben in Australia during the 1980s, Lester won a race, but was unimpressed by the trophy given to him, drawing the response from Brisbane Turf Club chief Sir Clive Uhr, 'Tell that bloke if he's so unhappy about the trophy we'll buy it back from him.' Lester reportedly accepted AU$100.

* ROLLING STONE Ronnie Wood is a Lester fan, 'My favourite big name horse was Never Say Die. It was a great Derby when we first saw the genius of Lester Piggott and I'll never forget that race or horse.'

* TRAINER David Elsworth had an opinion to air in a 1993 interview, 'Lester Piggott's a wonderful jockey, I agree. But, like some Flat race jockeys, he has exploited racing. He's a taker, not a giver.'

* TYPICALLY brief and to the point, Lester, who was deaf in one ear and had a slight speech impediment, was known as a man of few words, which – after being praised for riding a double in Dubai in 1993 – produced the comment ' Not bad, was it?'

* WHIP issues have always been controversial. In 1995 Lester said, 'We also have to remember that horses are bred and trained to run as fast as they can – and if it takes a few taps with the whip to make them do what they were bred for, so be it.'

* WILLIE CARSON, long-time rival, recalled in 1994, 'The old jockeys used to say you could not be sure of riding your horse in the Derby until you reached the start. Then you knew Lester would not be climbing on it.'

* WILSON PICKETT? Racing writer Steve Dennis told this amazing tale in his tribute to Lester, 'The Wilson Pickett story was given the mark of authenticity by the man himself in an

interview several years ago. England, the 1960s, Piggott at the stratospheric height of his renown. Or not quite, perhaps.

'Interviewer, "There are so many stories about you, and not all of them are true. Is the Wilson Pickett one true?"

'Lester Piggott, "[Almost a giggle] Yes, that one's true."

'Interviewer, "You were driving up the Finchley Road [in London], a hot day, you fancied an ice-cream, spotted a kiosk, went in. The girl behind the counter said, 'Aren't you Wilson Pickett?'"

'Piggott, "That's right."

'Interviewer, "And you said?"

'Piggott, "Yes, I am [laughing]."

'Interviewer, "But Wilson Pickett was a black American soul singer. And you're a little white English jockey."

'Piggott, "It seemed easier to say yes. I didn't want to get into a long discussion about it, y'know."'

* WORLD CUP-winning footballer Alan Ball recalled Lester riding the first horse Ball had owned, 'I asked Lester what he thought of it, and he said, "Glue!"'

* IT IS far from impossible that Lester's personality was shaped by a little-known incident from his childhood, chronicled by former jockey turned best-selling author Dick Francis in his 1986 official biography of Piggott. Lester was just seven years old when he was out riding with father Keith and they witnessed two single-engined aeroplanes from a nearby training base colliding overhead. Pieces of plane fell from the sky.

Francis wrote, 'Lester set off instantly to take a closer look. When Keith caught up Lester was looking at something laying on the ground. It was the body of one of the pilots. Before Keith could take any action, his son spoke. "He's dead."'

The two rode home. Keith and wife Iris anticipated their son having nightmares as a result of what he'd experienced. But, Francis continued, 'Nothing happened. Lester never referred to the pilot again and nor did his parents for fear of stirring up horrors.'

As Francis added, 'The cool head he took to racing was already in full command on the day he saw a man fall out of the sky and looked at his dead face with dispassionate interest instead of fright.'

* AS SO often, the great Hugh McIlvanney summed up a sportsman, this time Lester, in his inimitable fashion in 1991,

'With his face lined like a map of hard roads travelled, his capacity for pulverising put-downs and the inspired audacity of his jockeyship, he became one the most magical presences in sport over the last 50 years.'

KING CHARLES III

He made his debut as an amateur jockey, aged 31, in a charity race at Plumpton on 4 March 1980, finishing second on favourite Long Wharf – beaten by racing commentator Derek 'Tommo' Thompson riding Classified.

Four days later, HRH was fourth on Sea Swell in his first chase, run at Sandown. In October of the same year, Charles rode his horse, Allibar, to be second in an amateur riders' handicap chase at Ludlow.

Charles was subsequently unseated twice in the space of five days from his own horse, Good Prospect. He rode his sixth, and final, race at Newton Abbott on 21 May 1981, finishing ninth on Upton Grey, owned by his grandmother, Queen Elizabeth the Queen Mother; his career form figures read '242UU0'.

The former Prince told ITV racing presenter Brough Scott about the death of Allibar, who he had been riding, 'He crashed on to the ground. I held his head while the life drained out of it. I couldn't bear it because you see the life going out of his eyes. It nearly finished me. I've never had that happen.'

Charles had taken up racing for the first time – at the relatively late age of 31 – because, 'I wanted to understand what it was like from a jockey's perspective.' 'You have no idea until you do it what incredibly hard work it is.'

His first winner as an owner arrived when Richard Linley rode Nick Gaselee-trained Good Prospect to victory at Chepstow in early October 1981.

He and wife Camilla bred Carntop, and although the horse has yet to live up to Camilla's prediction of Gold Cup glory he did win a maiden race at Newmarket in 2015 and a couple of hurdles races in 2018 for her.

FREDDIE STARR

Comedian and former pop singer Freddie Starr was the owner of 33-1 1994 Grand National winner Miinnehoma. He was not present on the day because of commitments elsewhere, but gave an unusual post-race interview live on television to presenter Des Lynam, via a mobile phone, with viewers able only to hear Lynam's responses to what Starr was saying.

Starr, formerly the lead singer of The Midniters, had bought the horse in an unconventional fashion – bidding at the auction by sticking his tongue out at the auctioneer.

Speaking in May 2019 after Starr's death, Martin Pipe said, 'It's sad to hear the news. Freddie was a star of an owner, he really was. He sent us Miinnehoma in 1989 and his first words to me were, "I want to win the Grand National." I replied, "The horse hasn't even jumped yet!"

'Freddie had a few other horses with us too. He came and stayed, and there's a lovely picture on our website of Richard Dunwoody and Freddie with the trophy and me. We always enjoyed his company. He was great fun.

'Miinnehoma was a decent horse who finished seventh to The Fellow in the 1994 Gold Cup before winning the National under a brilliant ride from Richard Dunwoody – and he went back to Cheltenham to finish third to Master Oats the following year.'

Miinnehoma raced from 1989 to 1996, winning 11 of 25 starts, earning almost £250,000 in career prize money.

RONNIE WOOD

Rolling Stone Ronnie Wood gathered some dosh from his race horse Sandymount Duke, who won ten times for him between June 2014 and March 2019, including three and four straight win sequences en route. The versatile horse won on the flat, over hurdles and in chases.

The guitarist bred the horse, who was trained by Jessica Harrington and was entered for the 2019 Grand National, but was taken out after a setback.

He earned £111,000 during his career, but died in December 2019. Harrington paid tribute:,

'He was a brilliant horse, it's not easy to come across one like him. He was cantering up the gallop and went by me with his ears pricked just beforehand. He had never shown any signs of anything like what happened before.'

A respected artist, Ronnie has created pictures of Sandymount Earl and Joleah, both winners for him. He also painted the top-class Moscow Flyer.

But for all his pro-racing work, the rock star once complained, 'I got thrown out of the Royal Enclosure at Royal Ascot for not having a top hat!'

Quickfire Celebs Section

Celebrity chef HESTON BLUMENTHAL owned race horse Acolyte.

Actor SIR SEAN CONNERY'S Risk Of Thunder won Ireland's top cross-country race, the La Touche Cup, as 9-4 favourite in 2002.

Former swimmer SHARRON DAVIES was not really a racing fan, but did once have a date with trainer Michael Dickinson, 'All he did was quiz me about training techniques.'

Singer CHRIS DE BURGH named his race horse Missing You, after one of his hit records.

TV personality BEN FOGLE became an owner in 2010 with two-year-old Firebeam.

Ice hockey superstar WAYNE GRETZKY was part-owner of 1990 Prix de l'Arc de Triomphe, 15-1 winner Saumarez, and his 66-10 Golden Pheasant won the 1990 Arlington Million – while others have named race horses in honour of him – such as The Great Gretzky and Gretzky The Great.

Rapper MC HAMMER owned 1991 Kentucky Oaks winner Lite Light.

Actress ELIZABETH HURLEY was one of the owners of a Royal Ascot-winning horse called Memory, which was sold to the Queen in 2011.

Presenter and broadcaster JOHN INVERDALE'S Amour Propre was unplaced in Royal Ascot's King's Stand Stakes. His jumps horse, Make A Stand, won the Champion Hurdle in 1997, by which time he'd sold his share.

THE REV JESSE JACKSON was joint manager of the US Jockeys' Guild.

American actor GREGORY PECK, who won the Academy Award for his performance as Atticus Finch in 1962's *To Kill A Mockingbird*, was keen on racing. He owned two Grand National runners and was at Aintree in 1963 to see his 20-1 grey, Owen's Sedge, finish seventh to Ayala. Five years later, having won the 1967 National Hunt Chase at Cheltenham in June 1967, his

Different Class went close at 17-2, finishing third behind 100-7 winner Red Alligator.

Actor JOE PESCI, one of the stars of *Goodfellas*, owned the eponymous Pesci, who finished third in a Breeders' Cup race in 2004.

'A woman in our group backed a horse called Half Free because she had an on-off relationship, so she considered herself "half free". It romped in at 33-1 and since then I've always looked at the names of horses for clues,' said football legend SIR BOBBY ROBSON in 2005 on his favoured winner-finding technique. He was also a co-owner, together with IAN RUSH and JAN MØLBY, of Boogie Bopper, trained by Martin Pipe, who was a 9-2 Folkestone winner under Peter Scudamore in 1993. Sir Bobby also told of the time when he was England manager and goalkeeper Peter Shilton was also a racing fan, 'So we produced a video and had racing evenings, with Shilton as the bookie.' Shilton also owned a horse called Between The Sticks.

STEVEN SPIELBERG, the Oscar-winning director, co-owned race horse Atswhatimtalkingabout, fourth in the 2003 Kentucky Derby. He was also an investor in Biscuit Stables, Delaware.

Trainer John Gosden, who used to train horses for superstar actress ELIZABETH TAYLOR, told *Pacemaker* magazine in June 1999, 'I think she would have been quite happy for them to have been in the yard and never run.'

Former prime minister MARGARET THATCHER paid her first visit to a Flat race meeting in July 1990, at Newbury.

Rapper VANILLA ICE is a racing fan, who voiced much of 'The Real Story of Shergar', a podcast from BBC's *Sport's Strangest Crimes* series, which was released in June 2021. Ice's daughter was riding horses when she was little more than a toddler.

TV stars CAROL VORDERMAN and RICHARD HAMMOND were part-owners of Subway Surf, third in a February 2019 race at Ascot but a winner at Ludlow and Chepstow.

ROGER WATERS, once of Pink Floyd, has been a keen racing man, particularly over jumps, owning and breeding race horses – Lemony Bay won three times for him.

Racing Chat and Quirky Quotes

QUIRKY QUOTES

A journalist who appears now only to be remembered without a Christian name, Mr Phipps, is the man responsible for the currently ubiquitous practice of informing his audience by quoting the thoughts and opinions of jockeys and other connections following the running of big races.

Known on course as 'Phippo', and writing for *The Sportsman*, he started in 1900 to cultivate particularly jockeys, and to quote their utterings in his paper.

At first regarded as something of an outlier, gradually others realised that his reports were carrying information absent form his rivals and the practice began to spread. Here are some racing-related comments that are available to us as a result of Phippo's innovation all those years ago:

'Punters are cleaning up with hand sanitiser and then wiring into the Guinness. Last year an outbreak of equine flu almost saw the event cancelled. But even coronavirus, it seems, can't cancel the Gold Cup.'
- Leader column in the *Evening Standard* of 11 March 2020, reflecting that even a pandemic could not deter Cheltenham crowds.

'Got pissed.'
- Owner Andrew Gemmell, the blind owner of Paisley Park (named in honour of rock star Prince), telling *Times* writer Rick Broadbent (12 March 2020) how he celebrated that horse's 2019 Cheltenham Festival win.

'I can remember after a day's racing, people saying, "I hope you get cancer. I hope you die on the way home." Who cares? There's a block button for a reason.'
- A.P. McCoy, *Metro*, 10 March 2020.

Lester Piggott was famously ruthlessly self-centred when making sure he got on the best horses in the Classics, and was accused of depriving others of getting top rides as a result. Frankie Dettori has faced similar criticism but in May 2022 defended himself – and probably at the same time, Lester, too, when he reasoned, 'Someone said to me I was becoming like Lester, always kicking jockeys off horses. But there is a difference. I'm not kicking jockeys off horses; owners come to me and ask me to ride.'

'There are a few lads these days buying women's perfume as they think it smells better. But each to his own.'
■ Conditional jockey Ben Jones in the *Racing Post* on 26 January 2020, adding as his earliest racing memory, 'My first pony race, when I was so far behind, I thanked them for waiting for me to cross the line.'

'As long as it's not your neck or back you can usually be repaired. I didn't retire because I was injured, I just wanted to be doing a little better than I was.' Retired at 29, having 'smashed' his right shoulder 'to bits', meaning a year-long recovery, Williams also suffered multiple fractures of the left leg, while the bones of his left arm went through the skin in a double open fracture.
■ Welsh National-winning trainer and former jockey Christian Williams.

'A man, who must have been 14st, wanted to just finish a race. He actually pulled up with about a mile left to give himself and the horse a breather before continuing and he still fell off.'
■ Jockey Chester Williams (*Racing Post*, 23 February 2020) on his funniest racecourse experience.

'Racing is full of factions. My hope is one day a private equity firm might eye up racing and think the sport is ripe to be run by one streamlined company. I'm not a business expert but it seems to me racing needs to go down that track,' said *ITV Racing* presenter Ed Chamberlin in an interview by Lee Mottershead, in the *Racing Post* of 8 February 2020, in which he recalled the opening day of his role on 1 January 2017, 'The next day we were slaughtered. I always quote Giles Smith, who wrote in *The Times* that as a presenter I was as exciting as a self-assembly chest of drawers from Ikea.'

'Racing is all about life. People want to be able to watch sport because it makes them feel good, or they want to be able to compete. This is all part of the circle of life. You can't eliminate risk in anything. There is only one thing certain for us all, that we will only get so far and our bodies will fade and we will move off this earth ... racing is a sport and horses are athletes ... athletes get injured. We're flesh and blood and there is nothing perfect about anything in life. If a horse doesn't want to race they will let you know very quickly and people who care for horses and

are looking at them every day, they know when a horse is happy or sad.'
■ An unusually frank Aidan O'Brien in a 7 July 2019 *Racing Post* interview.

'Racing does not have the same place in society as it did. The raging love affair with the mainstream media is not even a flirtation in some ways now.'
■ BBC racing correspondent Cornelius Lysaght, as his departure from the role after 18 years was announced in December 2019.

'I reckon most trainers will be out of business in ten years time. It's all work and no reward, as you can't compete with the big guys running horses that cost 300,000gns or more in maidens with prize money of £4,000.'
■ Retiring trainer Alan Bailey, 80, in the *Racing Post* of 27 January 2020.

'The whip should be carried as an aid rather than something that needs to be applied. It would be absolutely ridiculous to take it away. I wouldn't take a horse over fences without one. Its use is something the regulator must manage alongside what the public will accept.'
■ David Muir, 21 years into his role as racing consultant to the RSPCA, speaking in the *Racing Post* of 27 January 2020.

'Yes, the toilet seat.'
■ Former champion jump jockey turned TV pundit John Francome's response on being told he had become 'part of the furniture of *Channel 4 Racing*', in July 2006.

'Not usually a sentimental man, A.P. [McCoy] insisted that when [talented hurdler] Get Me Out Of Here retired he would have a home forever with him and it is at McCoy Towers that he can be seen – beautifully stuffed in the corner of the hall.'
■ Alastair Down, *Racing Post*, 8 March 2015.

'My husband spent a couple of days running round after me like I was some sort of Egyptian pharaoh.'
■ Jockey Lizzie Kelly in the *Racing Post*, 22 October 2019, having broken her right forearm, while her left collarbone had come away from the joint.

'They call me Napoleon, but I'd rather it was Wellington.'
■ Born in Spain, French trainer Andre Fabre, who tends to keep himself to himself, to Sheikh Mohammed's racing manager of the

time, Anthony Stroud. Globe-trotting Fabre had played serious polo in Argentina. His Arcangues was a record odds (133-1) Breeders' Cup winner. Fabre also spent three years in Berlin as the son of a diplomat.

Trainer Robin Dickin said of his popular chaser, Thomas Crapper, that he could 'always rely on him to get me out of the sh*t'.

'The day he mounted another horse out at exercise and knocked the rider off was the day I thought "that's enough". It wouldn't have been quite so bad but the horse he was trying to mount was a gelding.'
■ John Holt, trainer of Number Theory, explaining why he took the decision to geld the 2012 Old Newton Cup winner.

'I thought then we had bought a sprinter, not a potential Derby winner.'
■ Celebrating three-year-old gelding Wolf Hunter's 2019 Jersey Derby victory, owner David Moon reflected that when he bought him for 10,000gns after he'd won on the all-weather over 6f at Kempton, he'd thought that would be the horse's ultimate distance. But he then was tried and won over 7f, then 1m 0.5f, then 1m 1f, 1m2f, and finally the traditional Derby distance of 1.5m. Unlike most Derby races, the Jersey version is open to runners of all ages – indeed, Wolf Hunter beat five rivals including nine-year-old Aussie Lyrics who had won the race three times previously, and 11-year-old Barwick, who had been runner-up in the Jersey Champion Hurdle on his previous outing.

'I'm sitting here with a big bacon sandwich and a bottle of champagne – and I know I can do the same thing again tomorrow morning if I feel like it.'
■ Great jump jockey John Francome explaining his decision to fellow top rider Terry Biddlecombe after earlier announcing his retirement from the saddle following a fall from The Reject at Chepstow on 9 April 1985.

'When you are slagged off by individuals who have no experience of what they are talking about then it really angers me.'
■ Kieren Fallon was not happy with comments by broadcaster Matt Chapman on *At The Races* during 2014.

'I give out a long-shot play every day at Gulfstream, and when one of those wins, you walk through the stands and people are

yelling, "You did great!" Then when you don't win, they call you a bum. That's the beauty of racing.'
■ Ron Nicoletti, US handicapper and race analyst at Gulfstream Park, speaking in November 2019.

'It's very emotional for me. I feel like pushing the wife over to one side of the bed and putting him in the middle.'
■ Owner Paul Barber after his popular chaser Denman finished runner-up in the 2011 Cheltenham Gold Cup.

'One evening, for a bet, I set my boxer shorts on fire. Unfortunately, I was wearing them at the time, and the scars took weeks to heal.'
■ The *Racing Post*'s 25th anniversary bash in 2011 proved to be a red hot event – according to Betfair media chief Tony Calvin.

'At first we were a bit like two dogs sniffing each other's bottoms. But although people kept telling me he was unreliable, money-grubbing and difficult to deal with, I found none of this to be true.'
■ Trainer Luca Cumani on jockey Keiren Fallon in 2011.

Impressed by the performances of jump jockey Lucy Alexander, the late trainer Ferdy Murphy said, somewhat anatomically inaccurately, of her during 2012, 'She's some rider – she's got balls of steel.'

'It's hard getting to the top. Once you're there it's just as hard, if not harder, to stay there.'
■ Multiple champion jumps trainer Paul Nicholls, speaking in 2012. He's still there.

Shortly after joining *Sporting Life* in 1990, journalist David Ashforth was tasked with calling trainer G. Richards to ask how his promising chaser Full Strength was doing. He was informed by Richards, 'Not reet well, lad. He broke his neck at Ascot three days ago.'

'As he was coming to the top of the stairs, I asked him what his problem was. As he opened his mouth, I just punched him one – all that anger that came from when he dropped me,' said US jockey Sophie Doyle, who had 28 wins from 249 rides in the UK in 2010, making her the leading female apprentice of that year before deciding to move to the States in 2013. She finally ran out of patience with a male jockey who kept causing dangerous in-race confrontations with her 'a few years ago' when they were both riding at an Indiana track. From that day on, declared Doyle, sister of 2019's top UK rider James, 'The guys in the jocks' room have respected me.'

'I saw it on Facebook the other day, "Why is it when you Google Sophie, she comes up as James Doyle's sister. Surely by now, it should just be Sophie Doyle?"'
■ Sophie Doyle, quoted in 2019.

'Well, he's come up here because he wants to be trained by a proper trainer.'
■ Sir Michael Stoute told Paul Hayward of the *Telegraph* in July 2019 what Henry Cecil told him after Shergar dropped his jockey and ran off one morning, ending up outside Cecil's then Warren Place yard.

'It is a pity his amazing legs cannot be patented.'
■ A tribute to 19-year-old hunter chaser Culmleigh Padre in the 1992 Mackenzie & Selby annual round-up of that scene. The horse had been running for an amazing 13 consecutive seasons. The same volume suggested that 11-year-old Flying Trove was now past his best and should be retired to 'hopefully be allowed to concentrate on rampant sex in future'.

Of Francolina, an eight-year-old mare who won a race despite being a 'remote fourth' when the three ahead all fell independently at the last at the Garnons track, it was said that she still 'only managed to hold a remounter by a length. She is basically hopeless.'

French Aggression, readers were told, was 'a well-known lunatic' – professionals jockeys refused to ride the 11-year-old gelding, who was 'as crackers at home as on the racecourse. Cares not one whit for his own safety.'

My Man Buck, a 14-year-old, could not 'run very fast' and was 'usually soundly trounced', so 'would probably like to put his feet up now'.

'We give race horses more care and attention than we give ourselves. If I could be an animal I would definitely be a race horse. They love doing what they are bred to do.'
■ *Love Island* star and ITV presenter Chris Hughes on 7 March 2020, defending racing over any negative public perception over the treatment of horses.

'He takes my breath away and when I call him Pegasus I call him that for a reason. He does feel like he has wings when he takes off. You end up floating in the air for more seconds than you think.'
■ Bryony Frost in the *Racing Post* on 7 March 2020, discussing her unique relationship with 2019 Cheltenham Festival winner Frodon.

Vets Jack Murphy and Sean Arkins of the University of Limerick announced research in 2008 which they said showed, 'The hair on a horse's head curls can tell you whether it is right- or left-hoofed, which in turn can help determine the direction a horse favours to race.'

The Name Game

There are a good number of candidates, but it is difficult to find a worse named horse than this one, who raced at St Albans in 1869. The horse had originally been named Rod in Pickle, but now appeared, glorying in a new title: Neurasthenipponskalesterizo.

Twenty years later an Australian horse, racing in Victoria revelled in the name Reverend Zacariah Stockdollinger.

Both difficult or unusual names, yes – but so was the much shorter nomenclature of the sprinter trained by current US handler Tom Amoss, who told someone asking just how the name of his Wrzeszcz, born in 2001 and owned by Richard C. Colton Jr, should be uttered, 'The number five horse!'

In 1971 the rock group America had a big with a single called 'A Horse with No Name' – and this may well have been the trigger by which owner Michael Baldry decided to call the unnamed two-year-old he purchased for £1,000, Myhorsewithnoname. Trained initially and for his two races in 2016 by Natalie Lloyd-Beavis, the next two and final ones, in 2017, were in the charge of Mark Hoad. In total, the horse had four runs, finishing ninth, sixth, seventh and 12th. This could also, completely accurately, be described as finishing stone cold last in all of them. That was the sum total of the horse's career.

My favourite race horse name is Cwrw. Possibly named because of the fun which could be had from non-Welsh speaking racegoers who, like me initially, would have had no idea it means 'beer' in the principality's native lingo. But even knowing what it means doesn't make it any easier to pronounce. In fact, Cwrw was a pretty decent race horse, who was foaled in 1809 and was best known for winning the 2,000 Guineas in 1812. His career lasted from April 1812 until September 1816, and he won six of his 26 races.

An Aussie horse of the 1990s had a Kiwi slant to his name – Waikikamukau – which could equally easily have been devised by an English-speaking lover of milk-producing animals.

And it isn't only horses who have tongue-twisting names. How about a Hungarian jockey, active in the late 19th century and winner of the 1883 Grand Steeple-Chase de Paris on the simply named Too Good? He was Georg Gobert Graf Erdödy von Monyorókerék-Monoszló.

But simple names can still be problematic – like the Australian runner of the early 2000s, Kennelle, or from 80 or so years earlier, an English stallion known as The Bastard, whose name was censored by prim Aussies to The Buzzard.

They can be somewhat disrespectful to the carrier of the name, too. How do you think the horse who won a race at Northampton in September 1751 would have felt, had he understood the meaning of his name – Dung Cart? Another winner, at the venue on the same day, was Why Not. Without a question mark.

Writing of trainer John Meacock, racing anorak John Randall said, 'His eccentricities, including giving his horses unpronounceable Persian names, transcended his lack of success and made him one of racing's great characters.' Vakil-ul-Mulk, who finished well down the field in the 1963 Derby, and Qalibashi were among his runners.

Keith Knight, in his Horse Racing Matters blog, declared, 'If I recall correctly John Meacock served in the army out in the Middle East and may have had the rank of major or captain. He named his horses after short passages to be found in the works of Shakespeare, translating the Bard's great prose into Persian, as if doing him a favour.'

Meacock, who trained from 1960 to 1971, died aged 85 in October 1999.

Names can, though, help when it comes to having a bet. How about American Jeff Thomasson, who was visiting Ascot in June 1996 and decided to risk £2 on a dual forecast bet, which came in when 25-1 Sea Freedom beat 100-1 Mirador. 'I liked the names of the horses,' he said when he'd stopped counting his £16,474 winnings.

Whether he'd have liked the name Wear The Fox Hat is unclear, however – but owner J.C. Wilson certainly did, which is why he called his two-year-old filly that and entered her for a race at Folkestone in 1995 only for the spoilsports of the Jockey Club to demand the filly be withdrawn unless her name was changed. Which it was – to Nameless, under which moniker she ran 13 times, winning twice at Folkestone in April and July 1995.

How those officials would have reacted if confronted by a two-year-old who began racing at Del Mar in the States in September 1991 called 'Honk A Wanker' is easy to imagine! And on a similar theme, British commentators had to be careful during 1994 when three-year-old Weigh Anchor was in action.

Some owners tried to fool the authorities over dodgy names – by spelling them backwards, with prime examples being Llamedos and Selosra. When trainer Alan Bailey tried to get

Norfolkinchance past officials, he failed – but had better luck with Finmental, which you should be able to work out.

Others are named because, presumably, their owners couldn't be bothered to waste time choosing a decent nomenclature – how else to explain Coolmore-owned 2012 Oaks winner Was, or the 2009 Irish 1,000 Guineas winner Again?

Both horses contesting a race at Newmarket's Second October Meeting in 1866 were named Robin Hood – and they were lining up against each other to decide which of them should keep the name. Mr Caledon's runner beat the one owned by Baron Rothschild, thus meaning that the latter was henceforth known just as Robin.

Many people like to bet on horses with names that somehow appeal to them – and when US actor Tom Cruise turned up at Goodwood in 2014 for his first visit to a UK racecourse he reportedly backed a winner called Shagah 'because he loved the name', said an ear-witness. One can only wonder why.

Commentators have all kinds of names to deal with but rarely has one taken advantage in the way Tom Durkin did when calling the runners home at New York's Aqueduct in January 1993. 'He's devoured this field,' declared Durkin, 'He just ate them up ... he absolutely had 'em for lunch,' he cried, as Hannibal Lecter stormed to victory.

Such matters of name abnormalities have gone on since the early days of racing. A horse sired in 1773 by the great Eclipse should have been named Potatoes – in itself newsworthy enough, but thanks to a stable lad whose spelling was somewhat erratic the horse was known as Pot8os or, apparently chalked on his stable door, Potooooooooos.

But it isn't only oddly named horses raising the occasional eyebrow – Bangor-on-Dee's 4.40pm race on 9 March 2005 may have had the longest single name ever attached to a race: it was the 3m Llanfairpwllgwyngyllgogerychwyrndrob wllllantysiliogogogoch Handicap Hurdle.

Racing Down the Years

1360BC

An inscription left by the chief riding master of the Indo-Aryan State of Mitanni in Mesopotamia in 1360BC was revealed in 1930 by a professor at the University of Prague, M. Hronzy.

According to the *Bloodstock Breeders' Review*, 'Horse racing is specifically mentioned in the document, which describes how the animals were first given a special reducing diet, accompanied by baths and gallops to induce sweating, while periodical purges of salt-water and malt-water were also part of the treatment.'

Hronzy deduced that in view of the methodical nature of the systems described they might have originated as early as 3000BC.

648BC

The 33rd Olympics reportedly included racing on horseback.

AD1154

The 1863 book *Horse Racing: Its History*, anonymously written, explained of the Romans, 'Their racing contests were not confined to the horse, but even asses were used as coursers, and ostriches also were made competitors! In their horse races, the jockeys rode in different colours. The principal ones were red, green, white and sky colour – to these were subsequently added yellow and purple.' The same book added, 'The earliest authentic evidence we have by written record of the fact of horse racing actually taking place in this country … is in the reign of Henry II, 1154–1189.'

1189

In 1189, claims the Encyclopaedia Britannica website, 'During the reign of Richard the Lionheart, the first known racing purse was offered £40, for a race run over a 3m (4.8km) course with knights as riders.'

1408

The King of Tibetan province Gyangtse decreed that 10–28 April each year should be set aside for prayer ceremonies, featuring among them horseracing.

1504

Racing was held at Leith, Edinburgh, on what was described as a 'long stretch of bare sand, also notable as the grim scene of executions for piracy', reveal accounts of the Lord High Treasurer for Scotland.

1540

Racing is recorded at The Roodee in Chester.

1576

There is, in the records of the Yorkshire town of Richmond, 'An entry in 1576 in the Corporation Coucher of a Cup for the Horse Race being in possession of the Aldermen.'

1595

'Two race tracks' were shown in plans of Doncaster's course.

1600

There was racing on Acomb Moor, 'which may very well have been York's first race-course, as early as 1600,' according to the 1920 book *British Sports and Sportsmen*.

1602

British Sports and Sportsmen reported that on 6 April 1602, 'We read with mingled feelings of interest and curiosity how there was a race at Sapley, near Huntingdon "invented by the gents of that county" at which Sir Oliver Cromwell's horse won the silver bell and Sir Oliver had the honour of the day. Mr Hynd came behind.'

1605

King James I paid the right royal sum for those days of £154 to purchase a horse expected to prove a champion. In the event, reported the Duke of Newcastle, 'When he came to run, every horse beat him.'

1615

In June 1615, the *Doncaster Corporacion* as it was then styled, announced, 'The race on Doncaster More hath brought and bred many caires and sutes wch tendeth to the great damage and prejudice of the Corporacion ... therefore for the preventings of sutes, quarrels, murders and bloodsheds that may ensue by the continuynge of the said race, it is agreed that the stand and the stoopes shall be pulled upp and imploied to some better purpose, and the race to be discontinued.'

Subsequently, however, the authority thought better of this drastic measure and racing continued as before in the following years.

1620

Historian Jessica Stawell discovered the earliest reference to racing at Burford in the Cotswolds from a report of a tragedy, located in the area's Register of Burials, which records, '1620, January 31. Robert Tedden, a stranger stabde with a knife by one Potley at the race.' Morbidly enough, the register also recorded deaths associated with a race meeting in 1626 ('slaine'), 1654 ('receive a wound and died thereof') and 1679 ('killed by a fall from his horse at the race meeting'). Oddly all three of these latter reports involved victims called William – Messrs Backster, a gent; and servants Howard and Clarke.

1622

A prize of £100 was at stake as a race took place at Newmarket between runners owned by Lord Salisbury and the Marquess of Buckingham.

1628

George Villiers, first Duke of Buckingham, was assassinated on 23 August 1628, five days before his 36th birthday. In his *A History of the English Turf*, Theodore A. Cook dubbed him, 'One of the most famous owners of this day … he married the richest girl in England, and owned the best racing stud in the country. He was but six and 30 when he was murdered after a short but sumptuous career, which apparently left very little benefit behind it to anything except the breed of English horses.' Cook added, 'Among his many betting transactions the loss of £100 over a race at Newcastle, to William, second Earl of Salisbury, is recorded.'

1629

J.P. Hore wrote that during this year, 'It was now agreed that the corporation and citizens of Salisbury should make up the sum of £320 stock to provide a cup to be run for yearly for ever at the general races there after the Middle Sunday in Lent. The prize obtained from this fund was a silver cup gilt with gold to the full value of £18.'

1632

Races are said to have taken place at Newcastle this year and in 1633, as well as at Ascombe Moor, Hambleton and Tollerton.

1634

A Whitehall dispatch from John Coke dated 14 March of this year declared, 'The King hath now declared that hee will remove fro' hence to Roiston on thursday next … This day the races for running horses wil bee come ended with the genral course for the gilden cup.'

1634

A letter dated 20 March of this year seemed to indicate an early example of a 'welcher' or at least someone less than anxious to settle his betting account, 'The Earl of Southampton, they say, hath lost a great deal of monie latelie at the Horse Races at Newmarket; but true it is, he hath licence to travel for three years, and is gone in all haste to France.'

1634

The Archives of Winchester show that it was agreed, 'The cittie shall yearlie provide a cupp of the value of £24, to be runn for at the race upon Wendesdaie in Easter weeke.'

1637

Popular writer and poet Gervase (or Jervis) Markham was very interested in horseracing and wrote considerably about the subject. On the matter of keeping a race horse properly fed, he recommended 'horsebread', giving a recipe, 'Take a strike of beans, two pecks of wheat, and one peck of rye; grind these together, sift them and knead them with water and bran and so bake them thoroughly in great loaves as a peck in a loaf; and after they are a day old at the least your horse may feed on them.' Closer to race day, though, cautioned Markham, 'Your horse must be wonderfull empty when he goeth to his course.'

1638

English officers serving in the Dutch army are said to have 'introduced the Turf to Holland for the first time' in 1638.

1640

Sheriffs at Chester gave a piece of plate valued at £13 6s 8d 'to be run for on Easter Tuesday'.

1641

A comedy, *Merry Beggars or Jovial Crew*, contained a reference to going to 'Hyde Park, to see the races, horse and foot'.

1651

In France the first documented horse race was held as the result of a wager between two noblemen. During the reign of Louis XIV, racing based on gambling was prevalent.

1654

Cromwell banned racing, for fear it might bring together crowds of those with royalist leanings and sympathies, resulting in political disturbances.

1655

Cromwell gave reasons for suppressing race meetings in his Declaration in Council of 31 October, claiming it was because 'royalists resolved to rise at the horse races, where they and their servants would come well armed, but were prevented by the prohibition of horse races'.

1663

With Cromwell gone, racing returned and in a letter, Thomas Ross, staying in Newmarket that March, reported, 'There is nothing but cursed noise, of matches and wagers boldly asserted with horrible oaths ... this day the first race was run between the Duke of Richmond and Lord of Suffolke who lost the day, and the Duke won an hundred pounds though in the morning hee got a very terrible fall in running a horse of my Lord of Tumonds, who tooke up the Duke bleeding at mouth and dead for a time, but hee got home, let blood, took Sperm-cete and went after dinner to see his horse run and immediately after to bed.'

1665

Sandymount racecourse in Ireland, founded in 1665, staged its final meeting in September 1859, after which the course became a track for human foot races.

1665

The original articles for a '12-stone plate' instituted by the King in 1665 to be run on the new round course at Newmarket on the second Thursday in October 'for ever' make fascinating reading: 'Eury [sic] horse, mare or gelding that rideth for this prize shalbe led out between 11 and 12 of the clock in the forenoon and shalbe ready to start by one of the same day.

'Eury horse ... shalbe bridled, saddled and shod, and his rider shall weight 12 stone; and eury rider that wanteth above one pound and a halfe after he hath rid the heat, shall win no plate or prize.

'Eury horse that rides the new Round Course three times over on the outside of the Ditch from Newmarket, shall leave all the posts and flags the first and last heats on the right hand, and the second on the left hand, starting and ending at the weighing post, by Cambridge Gap, called Thomond's Post.

'Whatsoever horse rideth willingly, or for advantage, within any of the said flags, shall win no plate or prize, but lose his stakes and ride no more; but if he be thrust by any horse against his will, then he shall lose only the heate; prouided he keeps all the rest of the flags, and come within distance.

'It is allowed for any horse to be relieved at the discrec'on of the owner at the end of each heat, and eury horse shall haue half an hour's time to rub between each heat.

'Whatsoever doth stop or stay any of the horses that rideth for this plate or prize, if he be either owner, servant, party or bettor, and it appears to be willingly done, he shall win no plate, prize, or bets.

'Eury rider that layeth hold on, or striketh any of the riders, shall win no plate or prize.

'If any horse, mare or gelding, shall fall by any mischance, so that the rider be dismounted, and if does his best afterwards to get within distance, and ride fair (which shall be determined by the Judges of the Field) he shall only lose the heat.

'Any of the Judges may weigh any of the riders at the end of any of the heats; and if he be found to have fraudulently cast away any of his weight, and want any more than his pound and a halfe, he shall lose the plate, prize, and stakes.

'If any difference shalbe about riding for this plate, which is not expressed in these articles, it shalbe referred to the noblemen and gentlemen which are then present, and being contributors to the said plate; but more especially the Judges, the Judge being to be chosen eury time the plate or prize is run for, by the major part of the contributors that are there present.

'Eury horse that winneth three heats shall win the plate or prize, without running the course.

'Eury horse that runneth for the plate or prize shall give to the Clerk of the Course 20 shillings, to be distributed to the poor on both sides of Newmarket, and 20 shillings to the Clerk of the Race; for which he is to keep the course plain and free from cart roots.

'The Clerk of the Race is to receive the stakes before any horse starts, and is to deliver it to the tenant for the time being, who is to give sufficient security, not only for his rent, but likewise to add such stakes to the ensuing plate or prize next year.

'Eury Horse, Mare or Gelding, that rideth shall likewise deposit 20 shillings for eury heat, which the winning horse shall haue; and the last horse of every heat shall pay the second horse's stakes and his own, which stakes are likewise to be deposited into the Clerk of the Race's hands before the horses start, to pay the winning horse his stakes eury heat, and likewise 20 shillings to the second horse, to save his stakes; but if there runneth but two horses, then no stakes to be run for but what is to add to the next year's plate.

'No horse that winneth not one of the three Heats shalbe permitted to come in and run the course.

'The plate or prize is to be run for the second Thursday in October, eury rider carrying 12 stone weight, at 14 pounds to the stone, besides bridle and saddle; and if any gentleman that rides shall carry weight in his saddle, he shall have liberty, provided he allows two pounds to the rest for the weight of their saddles.

'The Clerk of the Race is to summons the riders to start again at the end of half an hour by the signal of drum, trumpet, or any other way, setting up an hour glass for that purpose.

'No man is admitted to ride for this prize that is either a serving man or groom.

'Those horses that after the running of the three heat shall run the four mile course, shall lead away, and start within an hour and halfe, or else to win no plate or prize.'

1671

Hadn't happened before, hasn't happened since, but in October 1671 the reigning monarch, King Charles II, won a race, the Town Plate at Newmarket.

1674

It seems that after the Pilgrims landed in USA at Plymouth Rock in 1620, they may have brought with them the idea of horseracing, as in 1674 a 'Plymouth decree' was introduced stating that 'whatever person shall run a race with a horse of any kind in any street or common road shall forfeit five shillings in money forthwith to be levied by the Constable, or sit in the stockes [sic] one hour if it not be paid'.

1678

There was an unusual rule introduced at Blanford in Dorset for the May meeting, 'If any Contributor offer £15 for either Mare or Gelding before the Start the owner must sel[sic] provided there be two left to Run and the Purchaser is not to run him that year.'

1679

A forerunner of the form book was advertised for sale in the *London Gazette*, offering for sale a 'Register of Horse Matches' compiled by John Nelson of Newmarket.

1682

A race was run at 'New Markett', wrote Lord Hyde, explaining that it was over one and a half miles and 'had engaged all the Court in many thousand powndes, much depending in so short a course to have them start fairly'. However, when Mr Griffin, who was 'appointed to start them', 'saw the equall he said Goe, and presently he cried out Stay – one went off and run through the course and claimes his mony, the other never stird at all'.

1691

'Mrs Morte was the winning rider in a local horse race,' reported the *Chester Recorder* newspaper.

1698

Stipulations for a 'selling' race at Woodstock included that the winner should be sold for 40gns and 'if more than one Contributor be desirous to buy him, then to throw dice, the most at Three Throws'.

1699

In his entry for 28 February 1699, diarist John Evelyn noted, 'The Duke of Devon lost £1,900 at a horse race at Newmarket.' That is the equivalent of over £500,000 today.

1701

Soon to become the first Earl of Bristol, keen racing enthusiast John Hervey jotted down his diary entry for 6 August, 'Dear wife and I went to Nottingham to see ye Plates run for. Sir William Lowther's grey Mustard won ye Gentleman's at 12 stone that day, and ye next Lord Roos' Grasshopper won ye Town Plate at ten stone weight.'

1709

In September of this year there was a three-day meeting at York's Clifton Ings.

1712

Queen Anne's horse, Pepper, raced at York for the Gold Cup – which the Monarch had donated the previous year – but her horse was well beaten in two heats.

1714

Queen Anne's horse, Star, won a £14 plate at York on 30 July, galloping 16 miles during four heats, when there were 156 carriages at the racecourse, but two days later she was dead.

1723

Ripon reportedly staged perhaps the first race confined to female riders.

1725

The *Newcastle Journal* newspaper reported, without naming the month, 'On Tuesday 14th, the Ladies Plate of £15 value, by any horse. WOMEN to be the riders, each to pay one guinea entrance, three heats, and twice about the common for a heat.' There is, sadly, no record of the result.

1727

The earliest *Racing Calendar* was published, by John Cheny of Arundel, Sussex, containing details 'of all the Horse-Matches Run, And of all the Plates and Prizes run for in England of the value of Ten Pounds or upwards in 1727'. It also carried results from the 'Principal Cock-Matches'. In this year the richest racing prize on offer was the Wallasey (Cheshire) Stakes, worth 280gns, and it was run annually until 1732.

1727

Newmarket was the scene of a match in which, 'Mr Vane's Chestnut M, Bald Charlotte, 5 years, 18 stone, beat Mr Ashby's Grey H., Swinger, 17st7lbs, 4 miles, 200 gns.'

1728

Drummer, owned by Capt. Hugh Collyer, was the first recorded horse to win a race at Doncaster – the third winner of the day was the exotically named Sweetest When Naked.

1729

A race at Sunderland was in its third heat when second-placed Smiling Molly 'fell to her Knees – had like to have thrown her Rider, but Harmless, coming by at the time, his Rider Clap'd out his Arm, to clear himself of the Mare and Rider, and by that restor'd the Rider of said Mare to his Saddle and prevented his falling, but the other Mare by this time was near half a distance before, having in appearance the Heat in Her hands, but she took Offence at the People shouting and waving their Hats, and run on the wrong side of a Post, and though she immediately stop'd and turn'd back, yet it was too late, and the Grey Mare – Smiling Molly – won the said Heat, and consequently the Plate.'

1730

Racing at York's Rawcliffe Ings was postponed for three days as continuous heavy rains caused the Ouse to overflow its banks and flood the track. As a result the Knavesmire was chosen as an alternative course to use.

1731

The bodies of three robbers hanged earlier in the day, on 16 August 1731, were cut down to enable racegoers an uninterrupted view of racing at York.

In the same year, the first races for three-year-olds were staged in England at Bedale in Yorkshire.

1737

A ten-runner race over 4m for four-year-olds all carrying 8st 7lb was run at Newmarket on 23 April 1737, with Lord Godolphin's Lath winning comfortably.

1740

An act of parliament decreed that henceforth, horses could be entered in races only by their owner.

1741

Proud owners were invited by John Cheny of the *Racing Calendar* to acquire 'pictures of thirty six of the most celebrated horses that had been on the Turf, either in the form of prints at half-a-crown each, water colours at four shillings or, on canvas, painted in oil, at half-a-guinea each'.

1741

A publication known as *Cheny's Calendar* recorded the places in Ireland where horseracing had taken place that year: Ballynaslo, County of Galway; Bellair County of Antrim; Curragh of Kildare, nigh Dublin; Curlow; Darlington Queen's County; Down-Patrick; City of Limerick; Shanes-Castle County of Antrim; Trim County of Meath; Tuam County of Galway; Turlow-More.

1752

Possibly the first written reference to the Jockey Club was contained in an advertisement for a race to be run at Newmarket on 1 April 1752, 'A Contribution Free Plate by Horses the Property of the Noblemen and Gentlemen belonging to the Jocky [sic] Club at the Star and Garter in Pall Mall, one Heat over the Round Course, weight eight Stone, seven pound.'

The five-runner race took place at Newmarket three days later and was won by Captain Vernon's grey horse, Beau. This year was noteworthy also for an adjustment of the calendar, resulting in 2 September being followed by 14 September.

It is also the year in which the registering of owners' colours began at Newmarket.

1752

All racing fans know that the terms 'steeplechasing' or 'steeple-chasing' refer to racing over larger obstacles than those in place for hurdles races.

This originates from races run across country, often from one church steeple to another, perhaps the first of which took place in 1752 in Ireland between Mr O'Callaghan and Mr Blake. England's first equivalent appears to have happened during the early 1790s in Leicestershire.

But few will know where and when the terms come from. In January 1804 a race in Newcastle was referred to by the *Sporting Magazine* as 'Steeple hunting'. The same publication was mentioning a 'Steeple-Race' by December 1805.

The *Irish Racing Calendar* introduced a similar phrase in 1807, referring to the fact that during the previous year there had been a 'steeple-chace' run over a six-mile course at Ballybrophy. But by 1814 the Irish Turf Club wrote of 'a Steeple chase'.

1758

The race meeting scheduled for Burford was postponed as the 'Town of Burford is epidemically afflicted by the Small-pox'. However in July there was a re-think and towards the end of the month a three-runner race (after Sourface was pulled out) was held with Dormouse, White Legs, and Juggler, and the latter won two heats for victory.

Not so fortunate was jockey Tom Marshal, who fell from his mount and when he was 'taken up he appeared lifeless, and his Thigh Bone was stuck through his Buck-Skin breeches by the Violence of the Fall; but he is now in a fair Way of Recovery' under the care of Mr Batt, 'an eminent surgeon of Witney'. Phew! Except that on 31 October came a report that 'Tom Marshal, Riding Groom to Sir James Lowther, died at Allsworth near Burford – of a Mortification, occasioned by the Hurt he lately received upon Burford-Downs.'

Not such an eminent surgeon, then, perhaps.

1760

Racehorse owner Lord Ferrers was hanged at Tyburn on 5 May having murdered one of his own employees, following an incident at Derby races in early 1759, where Ferrers's mare won a £50 match against a Captain M's horse. After the race a row blew up when Capt. M suggested a re-match and Ferrers believed this had all been a set up to 'impose on him' or swindle him, with the connivance of his own 'steward'.

When he was tried, Ferrers was taken to Westminster from his Leicestershire home 'dressed in the habit of a jockey, in a strait-bodied cloth frock, jockey boots and cap'.

In these times the word 'jockey' usually signified an owner as it was normally they who rode their horses.

His body was handed over to surgeons for dissection.

1760

There was literally an outstanding performance at York races where, 'The famous Mr Johnson rode one mile standing upright on horse-back for 100 guineas. He was allowed three minutes to ride it in, but performed it in two minutes, 42 seconds.'

1760

The Rev Martin Madan, an important resident of Epsom, was no fan of betting, and in 1760 he 'was successful in using his magisterial authority in repressing gaming in the town during the race week'.

Not everyone supported this move, and some of the town's inhabitants were so indignant that, recorded the 19th century book *History of Surrey, Volume IV*, 'they burnt him in effigy'.

1762

Official colours were established for certain racing gentlemen and introduced by the Jockey Club 'for the greater Conveniency of distinguishing the Horses in Running, as also for the Prevention of Disputes arising from not knowing the Colours worn by each Rider'.

The longest-lasting of the originally allocated 17 sets of silks would be the Duke of Devonshire's 'straw-colour'.

1763

Huntingdon staged a contest which would have been difficult to price up: 'a Quarter of a Mile Match between a Gentleman and a Grey Gelding with one Leg tied'.

Who would you have made favourite? In the event, the gentleman won, as 'the Horse's Leg untied in running'.

1764

Jockey Joseph Rose, known in his day as 'the Flower of the North', found himself riding a horse called Favourite at Lincoln on Wednesday, 5 September. The very next day, he was booked to ride Young Davy, some 55 miles away, at Richmond in Yorkshire, then on Friday he was on Bachelor, a mere 125 miles further on, at Manchester. To get to these courses he had to hack there, carrying his racing saddle on his back.

1769

When his then unknown horse made his racecourse debut at Epsom in May, professional gambler-owner Dennis Kelly struck a bet with the phrase 'Eclipse first, the rest nowhere'. This signified Eclipse winning so easily that the vanquished also-rans would be too far behind to be officially placed. The bet was duly landed.

1769

A bay colt named Gibscutski (or Gibsoutsky in some sources), carrying 6st, beat the six-year-old bay mare Stilts, carrying 9st, over 6f for 200gns at Newmarket's Second October Meeting. It later transpired that the winner was a two-year-old, reportedly the first of such age to contest an organised race.

1770

The legendary unbeaten first racing superstar, Eclipse, won the Great Subscription at York, with witness William Pick noting, 'Eclipse took the lead at starting, and when at the 2m post, was above a distance before the other two, and won with uncommon ease.'

1770

One of the first, if not THE first, uses of the phrase 'the Knowing Ones' to describe racecourse shrewdies or well connected insiders appeared in a report from Burford races run on 28 July, 'The Knowing Ones never suffered so deeply. Such were the Vicissitudes of the Day that, at length many had hedged their Bets till they were certain of being great Losers whichsoever Horse proved victorious; and so fatal was the Catastrophe that the Downs were almost deserted the Day following.'

1770

Racing's first official Stewards with clearly defined powers are appointed – Sir Charles Bunbury; Lord Bolinbroke and Mr J. Shafto.

1772

George Washington (1732-99) first president of the USA, enjoyed attending race meetings, and recorded in his diary in an entry for 1772 that he 'lost £1/6 in bets at Annapolis'. In 2006, the Aidan O'Brien-trained three-year-old, George Washington, won the 2,000 Guineas.

1773

Mr T. Walker, on his own 'hackney gelding' and Capt. A. Hay's 'road mare' – ridden by Captain Mulcaster – raced from London to York, reported the *Sporting Magazine* in 1792, for a wager of an unrevealed amount. The event began at Portland Street in the capital, and ended at Ouse Bridge, reached first by Mulcaster in a time of 40 hours and 35 minutes, while Walker's horse 'tired within six miles of Tadcaster, and died the next day'.

As for the winning mount, 'The mare drank 12 bottles of wine during her journey, and was so well on the following Thursday as to take her exercise on Knavesmire.'

1774

Was Charles James Fox the first recorded professional racing punter? A letter from George Selwyn to Lord Carlisle suggested that he was, 'I hear that the night Charles sat up at White's he planned out a kind of itinerant trade, which was of going from horse race to horse race and so, by knowing the value and speed of all the horses in England, to acquire a certain fortune.'

1775

The stewards of Morpeth Races may have been 'woke' before their time, according to a report in the *Newcastle Journal*, in which the officials, 'desirous that all ranks of people might partake of the general satisfaction, so apparent at the meeting, humanely ordered five pounds of the subscription money to be distributed amongst the prisoners in the jail, an example worthy of imitation'.

1776

The first running of the race which became known as the St Leger two years later was staged at Doncaster, with five runners, and won by odds-on favourite Allabaculia over a 2m course.

1779

Now known as The Oaks, when this Classic race was first run at Epsom in 1779 it was named The Oakes.

1780

Nine runners lined up for the first Epsom Derby. It was won by 6-4 favourite Diomed, owned by Sir Charles Bunbury and ridden by Sam Arnull.

1783

A man with a very varied career, John Gully, one time-butcher, who became MP for Pontefract, was born on 21 August 1783. Gully had been a prize-fighter, made a fortune from coal, and owned the winners of every Classic race. His horses were trained at Danebury in Hampshire; he and his betting associates became known as the Danebury Confederacy. Gully had also been the landlord of the Plough Tavern in Carey Street, London. He retired from boxing in 1808, and took to punting. In 1827 he lost £40,000 when his 4,000gns purchase Mameluke did not win the St Leger. But, in partnership with Robert Risdale in 1832, he made £85,000 when St Giles won the Derby and Margrave the St Leger. In 1844, again in partnership, Gully won the 2,000 Guineas with Ugly Buck; two years later both the Derby and Oaks with Pyrrhus The First and Mendicant. Then, in 1854, he landed the 2,000 Guineas with Hermit, and also the Derby with Andover. He died in 1863.

1784

The government of the day proposed to introduce a tax of one guinea per annum on race horses, via, of course, their owner – and an additional £5 'on every winner'. There was so much protest at this that the idea was abandoned.

1788

Travelling from London to Epsom to see the Derby run can be a time-consuming exercise these days, due to traffic. Surely it would have been much easier and quicker back in 1788, particularly if you happened to be a royal personage, such as the Prince of Wales, who did indeed make the trip to see his Sir Thomas contest the race, on Thursday, 8 May. Contemporary reports show that he 'drove down in the morning from Carlton House in a carriage drawn by four horses with postillions, preceded by outsiders. HRH left town soon after 8am,' recorded the *Racing Illustrated*. 'The roads at that time not being conducive to any very speedy travelling, and reached the Downs, some half hour before the time set for the Derby to be run.'

The trip was worthwhile, as his horse won the race at odds of 5-6. He'd win it again next year, with the interestingly named Skyscraper, a 4-7 shot, but the Prince quit racing completely in 1791 following a scandal over the controversial running of his horse, Escape. 'The Prince sold his stud and gave up racing,' wrote Derby historian Michael Church, even though his own integrity had not been questioned, rather that of his jockey, Sam Chifney.

1788

Both 'runners' in a match race at York carried 30st in a 1m contest for 100gns. George Baker's grey horse was the 2-1 on favourite but lost out to Mr Maynard's bay mare.

1789

Racing journalist Steve Dennis wrote in his highly recommended 2021 book *A History of Horse Racing in 100 Objects*, 'When Eclipse died of colic in 1789, he was autopsied in an attempt to discover the reason for his superlative ability. It was found that he had a very large heart, which went a long way to explaining his athletic prowess, and thereafter his bones were reassembled and put on display as a curiosity.

'Later, his skeleton was periodically stripped down, transported around the country and rebuilt, with the consequence that along the way a few of the bones were lost and replaced by suitable bones from other horses. An inspection of the skeleton also reveals that his hooves are missing.'

Undefeated 18th-century thoroughbred Eclipse won 18 races, including 11 King's Plates. He raced before the introduction of the five Classics, at a time when 4m heat racing was the norm. He was undoubtedly the greatest horse of his era and the inspiration for the expression, 'Eclipse first, the rest nowhere'. He became a successful sire. His skeleton is on display at the Royal Veterinary College in Hertfordshire – whose resource centre is known as the Eclipse Building.

1789

Skyscraper won the Derby at odds of 4-7. Why he had such a name when buildings of such a nature were not common is unknown. It presumably meant something else to 18th-century ears.

1791

Cash, a yearling, was matched against the three-year-old Eliza over an agreed distance of 2f, 147 yards. The younger runner was getting 3st from the older in the race, run at Newmarket, and duly romped to victory. This was, said the 1926 *History of the Racing Calendar*, 'the first recorded instance of a yearling running.'

1792

Three runners contested a there-and-back steeplechase from Barkby Holt to Billesdon Coplow, four miles away in Leicestershire.

1793

It was described in 1896 as 'a circumstance perhaps unparalleled in the annals of the Turf' by *Racing Illustrated*. The publication was referring to the fact that in 1793 when races were commonly run for in heats, 'Mr Donner's bay colt, Meanwell', ran 14 heats for three Plates within five weeks – four at Stockton on 11 September; five at Boroughbridge on 3 October, in which the third was a dead-heat, and another five – the fourth a dead-heat – at Malton on 16 September.

Races of this nature were run in heats of two, three or four miles, so although the distance was not recorded here, it would have meant the colt running a minimum of 28 miles or a maximum of 56.

1794

A newspaper advertisement for the race meeting at Akra Farm racecourse, Calcutta, taking place from 16–18 January, offered 'breakfast with music provided in tents on the Course after the racing' with 'a Ball and Supper on the 18th'.

Also in 1794, the smallest-ever Derby field of four runners contested the race with Daedalus the 6-1 winner.

1797

Col. Cosmo Gordon had his gentleman's patent umbrella stolen at Ascot, and it is an indication of the scarcity and cost of such an item that he then saw fit to advertise for its recovery, offering a guinea reward to whoever 'brought it to the King's Head, Egham, within a week'.

1798

During a race at Chester, a horse named Hairbreadth bolted when leading and 'jumped the cords, and struck his head against an officer's helmet, being killed instantaneously'. The spike on the helmet apparently entered the animal's brain.

1798

In June 1798, the *Sporting Magazine* carried an intriguing story, revealing: 'A person who had been in the Nottingham work-house for upwards of 16 years as a man, with all the habits of one, dying last week, was discovered to be a woman. This woman had been a groom under the late Sir Henry Harpur, went under the name of Jockey Jack, had many times rode Sir Harry's horses a race over Nottingham course and was esteemed a good rider.'

1804

Racing had taken place in Farn in Cheshire since the latter stages of the 17th century, but was discontinued in 1804 when the racecourse was 'utilised for other purposes'.

1804

It didn't catch on, but in this year the *Sporting Magazine* for January began referring to contests between riders negotiating obstacles over a distance of countryside as 'Steeplehunts', elaborating, 'The mode of running such races is not to deviate more than 15 yards from the direct line to the object in view, notwithstanding any impediment the riders may meet with, such as hedges, etc.'

1805

'She rode side saddle in purple jacket and cap, nankeen skirt, purple shoes, and embroidered stockings.' This description is of Mrs Thornton (aka, according to some sources, Alice Meynell, daughter of a Norwich watchmaker and mistress of the colonel) riding Col. Thornton's Louisa, getting 4st, in a match race over two miles against Mr Bromford's Allegro, ridden by perhaps the greatest jockey of those times, Frank Buckle.

'A vast concourse' turned out to see the 500gns event at York, in which the female rider triumphed by half a neck.

Possibly fortunately for him, it is recorded by website Jockeypedia, 'Frank Buckle had an atrocious memory – he could not give an account of a race he'd just contested, nor could he remember the name of what horse he had ridden.'

Mrs Thornton's win was revenge for the match race run over four miles against William Flint, riding Brown Thornville, for a stake of 1,000gns on York's Knavesmire a year earlier when she was 22 years old and rode the colonel's Vinagarella, who was nearly 20 years old. Interest ran so high that 'only the fortunate presence of the 6th Light Dragoons kept the immense crowd under control'. Some £200,000 had also been gambled on the outcome and, said one report, 'the large sum involved may account for Mr Flint's ungentlemanly behaviour in beating his opponent'. Mrs Thornton's racing gear was 'leopard coloured and buff body, with blue sleeves and cap'.

It appears that Flint's winnings were not forthcoming and he posted the colonel as a defaulter before turning up at the Knavesmire and administering a sound thrashing.

1806

One of the first to endeavour to create a nationwide racing form book, politician, owner and gambler Charles Fox died. He once had 30 horses in training and would back them heftily, getting really involved while watching them race. One contemporary report described his behaviour, 'He placed himself where the race was to be most strongly contested. From this spot he eyed the horses; he breathed quicker as they accelerated their pace; and when they came opposite to him he rode in with them at full speed, whipping, spurring and blowing as if he would have infused his whole soul into his favourite racer.'

1807

A temporary stand collapsed at Perth racecourse injuring two lords, a duke and an earl.

1810

'As far as is known there was decided at Bedford in 1810 what was probably the first steeplechase over a made course,' declared Charles Richardson's 1927 book, *British Steeplechasing and Racing in Ireland*, which went on to explain, 'The distance was three miles, and there were eight fences of four feet six inches in height, with a strong bar on the top.'

Although 11 runners were entered only two went to post, 'The winner being a mare named Fugitive, who was ridden by her owner, Mr Spence. The other runner was a mare named Cecilia.'

It is said that 40,000 turned up to see this event, in which both runners 'had a certificate to the effect that she had been in at the death of three foxes in Leicestershire'.

Wrote the author, 'This is strong evidence that at that period cross-country racing was entirely confined to genuine hunters, and that race horses did not take part in it.'

Supporting this theory, Richardson referenced a contemporary sporting dictionary defining 'steeplechase' as 'a race over the country by hunters'.

1811

A reported 40,000 spectators turned up to see what purported to be the 'first race over manufactured fences' at Bedford, run over a 3m course in which four 4ft 6in fences were each jumped twice. Although eight entered, only two horses went to post, and Mr Spencer's mount beat that of Mr Tower – the latter rider collected on a bet of he'd made against Mr Palmer, constructor of the course, who wagered no horse would get round.

1813

Young Blacklegs, a four-year-old, was the winner of a six-runner weight-for-age steeplechase in County Rosscommon for a stake of £100, over 6m, over 'six walls each of five feet in height and several wide ditches'.

1814

Yorkshire breeder Henry Peirse, of Bedale, sent four of his mares to local stallion Comus, whose fee was 10gns. The mares were Rosette, which coupling produced colt Reveller; Rosette's sister produced colt Ranter; Albuera's new born was The Marshall, and Agatha's dam was Masker.

Mr Peirse kept the first two colts, while The Marshall was sold to Mr J. Powlett and Masker to Mr E. Petre.

That all four of these colts should line up among the 21 runners in the 1818 St Leger was surprising enough. That they should occupy the first four places, in the order discussed here, at respective odds of 7-2, 100-3, 50-1, and 13-1, was quite amazing.

1815

Owned by the Duke of York, Aladdin, unplaced in the 1813 Derby, won the 2.5m Ascot Gold Cup in 1815, as expected, at 2-5, but then came out the very next day, contesting the 6f Wokingham Stakes – running that, too, for the owner, whose Pointers had won the inaugural winning of the race in 2013.

1815

The Portuguese name of 1815 St Leger winner, Filho da Puta, translates as 'son of a whore'.

1816

It is frequently recorded that the 1836 Doncaster St Leger winner, Elis, was the first horse to be transported to a racecourse in a conveyance. However, this is probably incorrect as it is the case that in October 1816 a grazier from Worcestershire, Mr Terrett, sent his horse, Royal Sovereign, to contest the Newmarket St Leger, in his bullock float. The method of transport clearly suited Royal Sovereign, who won at 30-1.

1818

A history of London's White's Club listed from the betting book a wager dated 22 May 1818, whose precise nature seems unclear at this distance of time, but clearly involves racing. Judge for yourself, 'Mr Broderick bets 50gns with General Mackenzie on Sir John Shelley winning the Derby, against Lord Steward being married to Lady F.V. Tempest in six months from this day.'

1819

With 33-1 Antonio becoming the third successive St Leger winner sent out by trainer John Lonsdale, there was confusion as five of 14 runners initially missed the start, so the stewards ordered a re-run which took place without Antonio – who hadn't previously won a race and would never win another. However, the Jockey Club then overruled this decision, so Antonio retained the verdict.

1820

John Lonsdale trained his fourth successive St Leger winner as 7-1 St Patrick romped home in the biggest field to have contested the race – 27. Local landlord Mr Brown, of the Salutation Inn, backed his horse to finish in the first dozen, but it seems he was not a popular fellow as the crowd spilled over on to the track, preventing the horse from completing the course.

1821

Napoleon Bonaparte died in St Helena, where his 1815 exile had led to horseracing taking place in the grounds of his Longwood home, until his passing on 5 May. The horses were imported from South Africa, and the racing organised by Capt. (later Admiral) Rous, who went on to become known as the 'dictator of the turf' at the Jockey Club.

1821

William Taylor was 'warned off' for watching trials with a telescope.

1821

Dr Syntax won the Preston Gold Cup for the seventh successive season. He raced from 1814–23, winning 36 races, including five victories in both the Lancaster and Richmond Gold Cups.

1821

A 10m steeplechase in the north of England, from Stourton Church near Horncastle to Wickenby Church, was allegedly run over rough country, 'with upwards of one hundred and 20 leaps' being made.

1822

There were six races on the third day of the Royal Ascot meeting of 1822. The King arrived at 'soon after one o'clock' and departed after the third. The last race was not finished until 'nearly seven o'clock'.

1824

It is claimed that jockey Jem Robinson won £1,000 after laying a £10 wager at odds of 100-1 that he would ride the winners of the Derby – Cedric at 9-2 – and Oaks – Cobweb at 8-11 – which he did – and then complete a treble by getting married in the same week. The last leg of the three-timer was enabled when Miss Powell accepted his proposal.

1825

As an added attraction to the two-day fixture at Worcester (then known as Pitchcroft) beginning in early August 1825 and featuring the Worcestershire Stakes and their 4m Gold Cup, the race card advised: 'Mr Green intends ascending in his balloon from the Saracen's Head Bowling Green on Saturday at three o'clock.'

1826

For the first time, 'purveyors of that new luxury-food, ice-cream' appeared at Ascot, recorded course historian Dorothy Laird.

1830

The first St Albans Steeplechase was run, attracting 16 runners, and taking place 'from a point near Harlington Church to the obelisk in Wrest Park, near Silsoe'.

It was probably run on a 'two miles out and two miles in' basis and was won by Lord Ranelagh's grey, Wonder, ridden by guardsman Capt. MacDowall.

1831

The *Sporting Magazine* reported that the Blandford races had included the appearance of the sport's first female clerk of the scales. The reporter involved declared that he 'could not help thinking it rather outre to see a fair lady weighing the jockeys'.

1832

Sailor Dennis Collins was found guilty of high treason for the offence of throwing a stone at King William IV at Ascot. His sentence to be 'hanged, decapitated and quartered' was commuted to transportation to Australia.

1833

Born in 1833, jockey John 'Tiny' Wells, winner of eight Classics, once turned up to ride out wearing an Alpine hat with feathers, a suit in Gordon tartan and a pair of red Morocco slippers.

1834

Plenipotentiary, the 10-11 St Leger favourite, finished 10th of 11, and was rumoured to have been 'got at'. Contemporary reports suggested the horse looked 'more like a pig than a race horse' on the day. Some years later Plenipotentiary's travelling head lad confessed he had been bribed to 'lend' the key to the horse's box for an hour. Touchstone, the 40-1 shot, won the race.

1835

A large dog appeared on the course as odds-on favourite Queen of Trumps was poised to win at Doncaster, in September 1835, causing the horse to swerve, allowing Ainderby to win, landing a £2,000 bet for owner Frank Taylor, who sought out the canine's owner, bought the pooch and gave it a life of luxury.

1836

Reported racing writer T.H. Browne, 'A horse called Cyprian walked from Malton to Epsom for the Oaks, and then set off to walk to Newcastle-on-Tyne, where she won the Northumberland Plate after a tramp of some 300 miles.'

1836

Should anyone ever ask you when and where the first point-to-point meeting took place, tell them it was on 2 March 1836 at the Worcestershire Hunt meeting, run from Frieze Wood by the hills on the Madresfield Estate of the Earl of Beauchamp, to the centre of the Lower Powick Ham. Who won? Vivian, ridden by Captain Becher. And if they argue, tell them that point-to-point expert Michael Williams confirmed it in his 1972 book, *The Continuing Story of Point-to-Point Racing*.

The first such ladies' race followed 85 years later, in 1921, at South West Wilts at Motcombe, near Shaftesbury.

1837

The 17-runner Derby was started by flag for the first time. Phosphorus, at 40-1, won under George Edwards.

1838

At Melbourne's first race meeting, in March of this year, recorded Australian racing historian Maurice Cavanough, 'What the first race meeting lacked in refinements it made up for in enthusiasm. Bets were laid and paid in bottles of rum, with the unfortunate sequel that one successful punter imbibed so freely of his winnings that he blundered into the River Yarra and was drowned.'

1838

Queen Victoria attended Ascot for the first time, sitting in one of seven carriages which drove up the New Mile. She returned the next year to see the first running of the Ascot Stakes, won by three-year-old filly Marchioness, ridden by a featherweight jockey named Bell, the sight of whom amused the Queen to the extent that she presented him with a £10 note and asked him what he weighed. 'Please, ma'am, master says I must never tell my weight,' he stuttered back, to general amusement from those listening – in fact the lad weighed a mere 4st.

Victoria ceased attending the races following the 1860 death of the Prince Consort.

1839

William Noble, a 25-year-old jockey, was at the height of his powers, and rode the winner of the first Cambridgeshire Stakes, Lanercost. His father, Mark, had ridden the first winner of the Manchester Cup in 1816. However, the 25 March 1896 edition of *Racing Illustrated* carried a photograph of Noble, now 'in his 82nd year' – the oldest living retired jockey in the UK – and an appeal to readers on his behalf, as he 'has hardly any resources beyond a pension of £15 a year received from the Bentinck Benevolent Fund. Apparently the bank in which he had entrusted his savings, had gone bust.

'His wife is 84 years of age, and too feeble to attend to him. Lovers of the Turf will, we are sure, not refuse a helping hand.' Such sympathisers were invited to send in 'subscriptions for poor Noble, to two Edinburgh addresses'.

It was later reported that the appeal raised £49 11s. This amount is the equivalent of £6,942.04 today.

Noble died in September 1897.

1839

'Visitors from all quarters and by all sorts of conveyances have poured in upon us, by steamer, railways, coaches, chaises, gigs and waggons. Our inns have been crowded with the sporting fraternity of all descriptions. At one hotel they were thronged four in a bed,' declared one of the Liverpool local newspapers as 6-1 Grand National (or Grand Liverpool Steeplechase, as it was initially known) favourite The Nun failed to answer punters' prayers, finishing seventh behind 9-1 winner Lottery. During the same year a syndicate was formed to put steeplechasing on a permanent basis at Liverpool, with 1,000 shares offered at £25 each.

1840

'The term "deadheat", surprisingly enough, is only 113 years old,' declared *Racing Review* magazine in May 1953, 'having been first used by a writer named Hood in 1840. The word "heat", used in the sense of a preliminary warming-up race, is of much greater antiquity, being used by Googe in 1577.'

1840

The first thoroughbred horse brought to New Zealand was Figaro, who arrived in Wellington from Australia, where he was bred by the celebrated T. Icely of New South Wales.

In the same year, what may have been the first organised race meeting was arranged by the military garrison in Auckland.

1840

The 1840 Grand Liverpool Steeplechase was the second official annual running of what was to become known as the Grand National from 1847, run on Thursday, 5 March 1840, attracting a field of 13 runners.

It was recorded by the press at the time as the fifth running of the Grand Liverpool, but the first three runnings were poorly organised.

One of the 1840 runners, Valentine, took an early lead as his owner, Mr Power, had bet that his mount would be first to complete a circuit of the course. Reaching the second brook beyond the Canal Turn, Valentine looked sure to refuse, but his momentum was such that the horse stopped, reared, yet somehow corkscrewed, almost backwards, over the jump. The horse and jockey lost much of their momentum, but remained intact and were to complete the circuit ahead of the rest, landing the bet. The horse went on to finish third but gained immortality when, to celebrate the amazing, backward leap, the obstacle was named Valentine's Brook.

1841

Charity, 14-1, was the first mare to win the Grand National. Horatio Powell was her jockey.

1841

John Frederick Herring, born in 1795, had become a frequent exhibitor of his racing, coaching and sporting pictures at the Royal Academy, and was elected a member. Starting out as a coach painter, four-in-hand driver and artist, he was 19 when the spectacle of the St Leger of 1814, won by William, inspired him to try his hand at depicting race horses. He met with little success in this endeavour, but he persevered and gradually became famous for his portraits of horses, and notably for his picture of the 1849 winner of that race, The Flying Dutchman, which became an accepted major masterpiece. However, it was said that Herring's success went to his head and his subsequent extreme vanity did him no favours and led to a gradual unpopularity, which deprived him of much of his support in later years. It probably did not over-concern him, though, as in 1845 Herring had been appointed animal painter to the Duchess of Kent and he received a subsequent commission from the ruling Queen Victoria, who remained a patron for the rest of his life He died in 1865.

1842

Not content with their horse Gay Lad – some reports suggest Gaylad – winning the Grand National at 7-1, he was hauled out again just six days later to carry 13st 1lb in a race at Oxford, giving away 18lb to runner-up Roderic Random.

1843

Tom Oliver – some sources say Olliver – rode 12-1 chance Vanguard to win the 1843 Grand National, and such were his feelings for the horse that when it died, he reportedly covered a sofa with its hide.

1844

Red Deer was ridden in the Chester Cup by young jockey Kitchener, who had to have 10lb in his saddle to bring up his weight to 4st.

1845

Bookseller and publisher Henry Wright, based at 51 Haymarket, London, issued his first *Steeplechase Calendar*, detailing aspects of the sport since 1826.

1846

Racing in Natal, South Africa, was not only for thoroughbreds but also 'cocktails' of which 23 were in action at a meeting in

September, and which were defined as 'any horse of racing qualities, but not a thoroughbred'.

1846

At 20-1, Pioneer won the longest-ever Grand National, with the runners having to complete five miles after the course was wrongly flagged.

1847

Jockey John Day – known as 'Young John' so as not to be confused with his father, 'Old John' – was in the latter days of his riding exploits and partnering The Hero in the 1847 Goodwood Cup. He was so delighted at having won the race that, said a witness, 'he flourished his whip over his head in an indication of victory, universally acknowledged by his friends with loud shouts and throwing up of hats', while 'Old John', father to a dozen children, 'was almost delirious with delight, cutting all sorts of capers and dancing the polka in a style seldom witnessed amongst the most distinguished professors of the Terpsichorean art ... the shouts of congratulation were deafening and Young John was himself so overpowered that he was not only speechless, but the tears which fell from his eyes proved his sense of gratitude'.

1848

Lincoln racecourse came up with the idea of a new race called the Lincolnshire Handicap to be run at its meeting starting on Thursday, 5 October. The Lincoln, of course, was to become – and remains to this day – a popular event. But not in 1848 – the new race required a minimum of three entries ('bona fide the property of different owners') to take place, but that didn't happen, so neither could the race. It did, though, the next year, although only just, with Lord Exeter's Midia being the first winner, beating her two rivals.

1849

Ledgermain won the Cesarewitch – and within 24 hours of that success gave birth to a filly foal.

1849

The starter of the Grand National, Lord Sefton, attempted to recall the runners from a false start after he'd turned to make a remark to a jockey. His shouts were drowned out by the crowd in the proximity of the start whose yells of encouragement made a recall impossible. Despite Sefton having stated clearly that the race was a false start, the result was allowed to stand, with 20-1 Peter Simple confirmed the winner.

1850

The Governor of Hong Kong, Sir George Bonham, was the first in such a position to own a winner at Happy Valley, doing so when his Temptation obliged, and later winning one of the most prestigious events, the Canton Cup.

1850

Wrote *Racing Review* magazine in its July 1953 edition, 'The first bookmaker on record was a man called Ogden. Prior to 1790 owners and others backed amongst themselves. Starting prices first began in 1850.'

1851

Hoo knew that the racecourse of that name saw a four-horse dead-heat in April 1851 as Defaulter, Reindeer, The Squire and Pulcherrima couldn't be separated at the end of the Omnibus Stakes by the judge?

1853

West Australian became the first horse to win the 2,000 Guineas, Derby and St Leger in the same season, going on to win the 1854 Ascot Gold Cup. The horse was owned by John Bowes, who was winning his fourth Derby, and trained by John Scott.

1852

Charles Dickens was not a great supporter of betting on horseraces, and wrote on 26 June 1852, in his *Household Words*, 'Betting clerks, and betting servants of all grades, once detected after a grave warning, should be firmly dismissed.'

1855

A rarity, even in those days, as the judge called a four-way (Overreach, Lady Golightly, Gamester, The Unexpected) dead-heat in a five-runner, two-year-old race at Newmarket in October, 1855.

1856

Yearling racing reappeared this year and continued for a few years afterwards. Also in 1856, the so-called 'dictator of the turf', Admiral Rous, accurately called betting 'a necessary adjunct to racing'.

1857

Punters hoping to have a wager on the upcoming December races at the Wanganui course in New Zealand were advised by the local *Wellington Chronicle* newspaper, 'By some accident we cannot account for, a very spirited account of the Wanganui Race Fund and the probable chance of the horses has been mislaid. We offer our sincere apologies.'

1857

The Grand National was won by Emigrant, ridden by Charles Boyce who was effectively one-armed as he had one of his two strapped to his body following a hunting accident. Boyce's chances were also helped when he spotted a way of improving his victory hopes by galloping along a towpath as he approached the Canal Turn – a move subsequently prevented by the erection of flags.

1857

The Mariners Stakes was included on the card at Hartlepool in which the horses had to be 'ridden by captains of vessels'. Three washed along and Capt. Thomson sailed home, beating Capts. Ling and Parsell, and winning the £10 prize.

1858

A witness account of racing in Hong Kong described one of the races at Happy Valley, 'Thirteen started and four or five of the riders fell off first go; the merriment of the spectators baffles all description. However the dismounted cavaliers showed great pluck and got up grinning as though nothing had happened. Four of the riders kept well together and the winner came in in gallant style, amid great applause.'

1859

Racing over hurdles began in India at Jullundur, Meerut and Lucknow. Yearling races were banned in Britain.

1859

Musjid, the 9-4 favourite, won the Derby, run on Wednesday, 1 June, with 20-1 Ticket-of-Leave placed second. However, connections of Marionette, a 22-1 chance, were convinced they had finished runner-up. They persuaded the judge that he had made a mistake, and two days later, after the Oaks had been run, a meeting took place, following which a notice was posted, 'The stewards hereby declare Marionette to be the second horse in the Derby Stakes and that Ticket-of-Leave was placed second by mistake.' The notice was signed, 'Beaufort; A. Heathcore; H.J. Rous; C.H. Carew. June 3rd, 1859.'

1860

Owner James Merry was able to live up to his surname – as he was said to have won £500,000 on his horse, Thormanby, when he won the Derby.

1860

The Queen's Plate, now Canada's oldest thoroughbred horse race, was founded in 1860. It is also the oldest continuously run race in North America. On 1 April 1859, the Toronto Turf Club petitioned Queen Victoria to grant a plate for a race in Ontario. Her Majesty granted the petition of the little turf club in the boisterous Upper Canada community (the population of Toronto was 44,425) and offered as an annual prize, 'a plate to the value of Fifty Guineas'.

The race's website notes, 'The Queen's Plate is not a plate … About it not being a Plate; King Charles II began awarding silver plates as racing prizes in the 17th century at Newmarket, the size of the plate indicating the value of the race. But the practice became outmoded, perhaps as variety was sought in the prize. Other pieces of silver were instituted as awards and then other metals were used. Nowadays, The Queen's Plate is actually a gold cup, about a foot high.'

1861

The *Airdrie Advertiser* campaigned to have racing banned locally in 1861, citing as its reasons, 'Fast youths, fancy men, gamblers, blacklegs and women of easy virtue,' which some may say could have doubled up as a list of attractions.

1862

A nine-race card at Newmarket's October meeting saw all nine favourites winning.

1863

The first £1,000 prize money race was run for in New Zealand at Silverstream in Dunedin, where the local champion, Lady Bird, defeated top Australian raider Mormon over 3m. The visiting Aussies who lumped on at 2-1 were reportedly 'most crestfallen'.

1864

The four jockeys riding in Salisbury's Stonehenge Plate were dumbfounded when they discovered they would have to run the race again as the judge had not been in place to confirm an official result. So they did – producing the same finishing order, only an official one this time.

1864

Perth racecourse's future seemed to be in doubt as the *Sporting Gazette* newspaper attended a meeting and declared it 'very deficient in legitimate racing and, as a matter of course, a considerable amount of "squaring" took place – unless there is some great change in management we have seen the last of bona fide racing at Perth'. Racing struggled on at the North Inch until 1892, but then relocated to Scone Palace Park in 1908.

1865

The first steeplechase recorded in India was run at Rawalpindi.

1865

A letter appeared in the *Bell's Life* newspaper, in which the writer declared, 'I do object to English racing, as the world generally understands it, being degraded, and sincerely trust that we have heard the last of proposals for £1,000 stakes to be run at "gate money" meetings in the neighbourhood of the Metropolis, where the locality, for the time being would inevitably be swamped with the scum and scoundrelism of London at the expense of order and decency, and the reputation of the national pastime.'

1866

The first serious racing bookmaking enterprise in America, where pool betting had been the normal method of placing bets, was introduced by a Philadelphia company called Sanford, Sykes & Eaves – who had been doing business mainly on cricket, as well as regattas and trotting.

1868

Queen Victoria was not amused that her son, the 27-year-old Prince of Wales, later to become King Edward VII, was going to the Punchestown races in Ireland, writing to him, 'I much regret that the occasion should be the races as it naturally strengthens the belief, already too prevalent, that your chief object is amusement.' The Prince came up with an appropriate reply, 'I do not go there for my amusement, but as a duty.' Of course.

1868

Mr Youngman rode Woodbury Hill to win the principal steeplechase run at Bristol – only to be objected to by the runner-up on the grounds that the winning jockey 'was not qualified to ride as a gentleman'.

The controversy was sent up to the stewards of the Grand National Hunt Committee who duly debated the affair – and upheld the objection.

Racing at Bristol continued until 1888.

1869

In the UK there were 155 jumps venues, possibly a record, which staged 695 races during the year.

1870

An unknown apprentice won on one of his three rides at Perth – Fred Archer was barely a teenager at 13.

1870

Racing ceased taking place on the sands at Redcar.

1870

The then Duke of Edinburgh, Prince Alfred, visited Australia to see the Melbourne Cup. At the course he was introduced to John Tait, owner of the favourite, Pyrrhus, who told the Royal he was confident his horse would win 'easily'. Taking the tip, the Prince promptly staked £50 – reckoned to be the equivalent of £6,341 in 2022 – then watched as Pyrrhus was well beaten as a horse called Florence won from the front. Florence was also owned by Mr Tait.

Whether the Prince tried to recoup his losses on the Cup itself is not known, but there was a bizarre story to the winning horse, Nimblefoot. Publican Walter Craig owned Nimblefoot. But a few months before the 1870 race, run on 10 November, Craig dreamed of a horse in his colours winning the cup but with its jockey wearing a black armband. As a result, Craig became convinced that Nimblefoot would win, but that he would not be alive to see it happen. Craig died on 17 August from gout and pneumonia. His dream was recounted in *The Age* newspaper the day before the Cup. Sure enough, in a close finish, 12-1 chance Nimblefoot, now owned by Craig's widow, and whose jockey J. Day was wearing a black armband, beat Lapdog in a tight finish.

1871

Lord Poulett, who owned chaser The Lamb, had a dream that the horse won the Grand National, ridden by Tommy Pickernell. When he awoke, in December 1870, he set about booking Tommy to partner the horse in the big race, and they duly won in 1871, running at 5-1.

1871

James E. Kelley, a bookmaker from New York, launched a 'winter book', which presumably was an ante-post market, on the 1871 Belmont Stakes, and became known as 'the pioneer specialist in horseracing'.

1872

A report of racing at Stockton-on-Tees in 1872 saw the correspondent noting, 'I never saw any track in more deplorable condition than that at Stockton when Juga upset the odds betted on Lord Zetland's Khedive through a perfect sea of mud. The condition of the jockeys, particularly those who had ridden slow horses, when they came back to scale after each race, was sufficient to invite compassion, and many a smart jacket must have been spoilt during that memorable week.'

1872

The answer had been up in the air, until May 1872, when Eadweard James Muybridge, a pioneering photographer, who had adopted the name 'Eadweard' as the original Anglo Saxon-form of 'Edward' and the surname 'Muybridge' (for Muggeridge) believing it to be similarly archaic, set about determining once and for all whether, and if so, in what fashion, a race horse's hooves all lost contact with the ground during any phase of a trot or run.

Explained *Sporting Life* in 1951, 'Early experiments made at Sacramento, California, in May 1872, proved, despite the crudity of the apparatus, that they do, but not at the point suggested in old engravings (with front and back legs off the ground together in the same positions) – which in any case is physiologically impossible.

'Later, Muybridge decided to make his evidence conclusive. At Palo Alto, San Francisco, he erected a battery of 24 cameras side by side; each shutter was operated by an electro-magnet which in turn was actuated by a thread drawn across the path of the horse. As the horse trotted past the cameras, it broke thread after thread, thus making 24 consecutive exposures and proving beyond doubt that the four hooves are off the ground when bunched together in the suspension.'

1873

The reported crowd at the Melbourne Cup was 70,000 – which, declared Aussie authors Cavanough and Day in their *Cup Day* book , 'On a population basis, if the same proportion of people in England attended the Derby that year, over four million people would have been present at Epsom Downs.' The 3-1 shot Don Juan won the Cup that year, in a record time of 3min 36sec – despite protests that the four-year-old was a year older than that and was a ringer.

1874

The Lincoln, one of the 'Spring Double' races, together with the Grand National, was in danger of disappearing from the calendar in 1874, until bookmakers had a whip-round to fund the £1,000 purse. Prize money went to Tomahawk, beating 34 rivals, under 17-year-old Fred Archer who this season would become champion jockey for the first time.

1874

'It is unfortunate that the noble and useful sport of horseracing cannot exist and be enjoyed without giving birth to, as a class, the most unmitigated scoundrels that are to be found in the world,' so wrote the May 1874 *Dublin University Magazine*.

1874

Jockey 'Tod' Sloan was born this year. His Christian name was James, but as a child he was nicknamed Toad, because of his diminutive size, which perhaps accounts for his first employment as an assistant to a balloonist at county fairs, but he soon became attracted to racecourses at which his size was a benefit. His short legs resulted in him adopting what would become famous as the 'monkey on a stick' style of riding, which also became extremely effective for him. Somewhat fastidious and arrogant as his success grew, he came to England to ride and in 1898 rode 166 winners from 362 rides – a 46 per cent win average, including a five-wins-from-five-rides day at Newmarket on 30 September (other reports suggest he also did so on 28 May at Gravesend). Back in the US he announced to newspaper reporters that he would repeat that feat at Ingleside, California – which he achieved on 21 March 1899.

Returning to England the following year, he won several important races including the 1899 1,000 Guineas aboard Sibola, and in 1900 the Ascot Gold Cup, riding Merman for owner Lillie Langtry. In 1900, Edward, Prince of Wales, offered Sloan the job to ride for his stable in the 1901 racing season. For whatever reason – because it was true, or because many were jealous of his success – Sloan's racing career was spectacular, and it was relatively short, ending under a cloud of suspicion, of which there seemed to be little proof, that he had been betting on races in which he had competed. Advised by the Jockey Club that they would not renew his licence, he never actually rode for the Prince of Wales. The British ban was maintained by American racing authorities, and Sloan's riding career came to an end. There are reports that he tried his hand at training in England but was asked to leave the country when the First World War broke out as he was an 'undesirable alien'. He died in 1933.

1875

The Rev John William King, born in 1793, became a vicar in Ashby-de-la-Launde, Lincolnshire, in 1822. His father died, leaving him a stud, with instructions that he should never sell it. So he bred and raced the horses, hiding behind the name 'Mr Launde', but never once attended a race meeting, nor ever placed a bet. His colt, Manganese, won the 1856 1,000 Guineas, and in 1874 his filly Apology cleaned up at three Classics, the 1,000 Guineas, Oaks and St Leger. He died in 1875.

1876

Prince Gustav Batthyany, a leading owner of the day, launched a petition in 1876, which was presented to the Jockey Club on behalf of owners and trainers who were fearful that closely guarded information, or 'training reports' about their horses, was being leaked out to 'certain cheap spori'ng newspapers'.

Declared the petition, 'This information is largely obtained from servants, boys and even apprentices, who attempted to violate their master's secrets by an organised staff of paid horse-watchers and touts who are, as we believe, maintained at the chief training establishments in the country at the expense of those papers.

'The result of their efforts is to corrupt and demoralise, and in many cases to cause the discharge and ruin of servants and boys in training stables and a further result is the entire destruction of confidence between the employer and the employed.

'It is against this system, so dubious, so dishonourable in practice, so injurious to owners and trainers, and so entirely subversive of the morality and best interests of the turf that we earnestly protest and we trust that the Jockey Club will take such immediate steps as may be desirable to arrest its future progress.'

Sounds like privileged buck-passing to me!

1877

A Victorian traveller, Mrs Brassey, was in Hong Kong attending the last day of the race meeting there. She described the Happy Valley course as having a thatched roof, verandahs, sun blinds, and 'the most luxurious basket-chairs one could possibly desire'. Attendance was 'very large' and most of the horses were 'little Chinese ponies with European riders whose feet almost touched the ground'.

1880

Visiting from England, John William Coleman was not over-complimentary about his first experience of South African racing, writing of his trip to Durban's course, 'If a person wishes to witness debauchery and a set of semi-intoxicated soft-brained noodles, misnamed men, I would counsel that person to frequent the course.'

1880

A meeting run at Gate Pa, Tauranga, in New Zealand, offered a living winner-tipping service, known as 'Canaries and Monkeys'. 'Punters paid out 2/6d and a canary or monkey would pick a number out of a hat,' explains a contemporary report.

1880

The Duke of Omnium, in 1880's *The Duke's Children* by Anthony Trollope, declares, 'Races ! A congregation of all the worst blackguards in the county, mixed with the greatest fools!'

1882

Newmarket became the property of the Jockey Club. During the same year, all five Classic races were won by fillies – Shotover took the 2,000 Guineas and Derby; St Marguerite the 1,000 Guineas, Geheimniss the Oaks and Dutch Oven the St Leger.

1883

Readers met Prince Gustav Batthyany in our 1876 section. Fast forward seven years in Newmarket, shortly before Galliard, a son of the Prince's beloved horse Galopin, who won the 1875 Derby, was due to run in the 2,000 Guineas. Recounted the Duke of Portland, 'About half an hour before the race Prince Batthyany was walking to the Jockey Cub luncheon room at the stand at Newmarket, and I was walking with Lord Charles Beresford just behind him. When he reached the small flight of steps leading to the room he fell headlong. Lord Charles and I immediately picked him up, but he was dead, quite dead, and I am convinced that he was dead before he hit the ground.'

The Duke had a theory about this fatality, 'His death may very probably have been due to the excitement with which he was looking forward to the great race in which Galliard was a competitor.'

With Fred Archer on board, Galliard went off at 9-2 against 14 opponents, prevailing by a head.

The Duke's theory was probably accurate – as Batthyany had a heart condition that enforced the early retirement of Galopin at the end of the 1875 season, as it was feared that the excitement of watching him race again could put the Prince's life at risk.

1884

Lady Anne Bentinck, a 92-year-old race horse owner, died in 2008. She left trainer Sir Mark Prescott an unusual gift – the skin of legendary 19th-century race horse St Simon, 1884 Ascot Gold Cup winner and great sire, owned by her grandfather.

In the same year, the Hong Kong Jockey Club was founded, succeeding the previous authority, the Racing Committee.

1885

Irish Grand National winner Billet Doux was beaten later in the season in Punchestown's Conyngham Cup by outsider John Kane, owned and trained by County Kildare farmer William Hanway, who explained that it was his practice to let his horses loose in a large field, and then send collie dogs into the same field to chase the horses, claiming it to be 'a performance both horses and dogs enjoy so much that they get plenty of it'.

1885

The Bard, a two-year-old, won 16 races during the season – one of them a walkover – setting a British record in the process.

1886

Blanchard won at Newmarket in October 1886, giving multiple champion jockey Fred Archer his 2,748th winner. No one guessed it would also be his final winner. Ten days later he committed suicide, shooting himself.

1886

Born on 1 November in Ontario, Canada, to a Mancunian father, jockey Fred Herbert joined a troupe of circus acrobats at the age of eight, only to break his arm when falling from a trapeze. He then ran away and ended up as a jockey in Louisville, Kentucky – where he rode a winner called Bananas and Cream when he was a mere ten (or 12, depending which account you believe) years old. In 1909 he rode 227 winners in Canada then began travelling – and riding winners in 16 countries, including India, Italy, Australia, France, Egypt and England, coming to England in 1912, with a winner of the Kentucky Derby (Donau, 1910) to his credit, and a nickname of 'Brusher'. He announced his retirement in 1947.

1887

Mornington Cannon, just 13, rode his first winner, Flint, at Salisbury in May 1887, and was rewarded by trainer Charles Morton, who gave him a sovereign and suggested he should use it to buy sweets.

1887

Legendary gambler Ernest Benzon – whose full name was Henry Ernest Schlesinger Benzon, popularly known as 'The Jubilee Plunger' – was said by the *New York Times* to have 'earned fame by gambling away $1,250,000 in 1887'.

An article about him in a 1948 publication, written by Terence Stanford, was less than glowingly complimentary, and started off by calling him 'Triple Crown "mug"', continuing, 'This greasy-faced lard-headed oaf should not have been allowed to play snakes-and-ladders for penny points, let alone match his wits against some of the shrewdest men of the turf.

'He backed unheard-of horses for unheard-of sums. The slightest whisper of a tip – however ill-informed the source – was sufficient to send him plunging to the rails, prepared to bet his boots.

The bookmakers of his time almost declared a day of mourning when finally – and deservedly – he went broke.'

In 1890 his autobiography was published in the UK as *How I Lost £250,000 In Two Years*, in which he revealed that when he came of age after his parents had died when he was very young, 'I had a quarter of a million at my disposal.'

He bought four horses in, and to race on, the Isle of Wight, revealing that he expected 'to have won a good stake' on his horse, Eve, but instead, 'I dropped about £3,000 at the meeting.'

He continued to explain how he managed to gamble away huge sums, but did say, 'I freely admit that the Jubilee Year was one big mistake so far as I was personally concerned.' However, 'Should I ever again come into money, I do not believe that the experience of that, to me, ill-fated period will prove to have been otherwise than advantageous.'

After losing nearly all of his inherited money, Benzon was granted £400 per annum by the family trustees and he moved abroad, returning to live in London in 1905 and dying in December 1911.

In one of the notices of his death it was written, 'Of the generation of foolish young men of the last half-century, who dissipated large fortunes, Benzon was the most foolish.'

1888

Ayrshire, the 5-6 favourite, won the 1888 Derby, owned by the 6th Duke of Portland, who later related the story behind the winner's dam, Atalanta, purchased from Lord Rosslyn, who in turn had acquired the mare when she 'had met with some injury and could hardly stand up.

'A lot of bargaining took place and Rosslyn eventually paid 7s 6d cash, adding a wheelbarrow, and a matrimonial engagement for a prize sow – I hardly suppose that the dam of a future Derby winner ever before or afterwards changed hands under such peculiar circumstances.'

1888

Playfair won the Grand National as a result of his jockey, Mawson, being pulled back into his saddle by fellow rider Arthur Nightingall after Playfair had pecked badly at one of the fences.

1889

Owned by Winston Churchill's father, Lord Randolph, and named by Winston's mother, Lady Churchill, L'Abbesse de Jouarre after a 13th-century French abbess, commonly known among racing followers as 'Abscess on the Jaw', was a 20-1 winner of that year's Oaks. Lady C herself would recall being on a Thames launch on the day, 'On my asking the lock-keeper which horse had won the big race he replied to my great delight and amusement, "The Abesse on the Jaw."'

1889

Discussing jockeys in his *Ethics of the Turf*, author J. Runciman declared them to be, 'Skinny dwarfs whose leaders are paid better than the greatest statesmen.'

1889

Trayles, third in the Cesarewitch the previous season, won the Ascot Gold Cup, together with, the day after, the Alexandra Gold Plate, then the Goodwood Cup, a unique treble. The horse's wealthy owner was also unique – Warren de la Rue, the grandson of Thomas de la Rue, founder of the de la Rue printing company, which produced Britain's stamps, and those of her colonies as well. He owned a house in London's Regents Park, in which he had a special lift installed for transporting his false teeth down to be cleaned by his valet. He acquired two 15-bedroom houses in Tenby, but had them knocked down and applied for permission to replace them with a self-designed home named 'Trayles', which was duly granted, only for de la Rue to change his mind shortly after, before resuming the plan and having a 'magnificent, fine Edwardian residence' constructed and named after his equine hero, featuring a specially commissioned, fine sculptured head of Trayles above the main doorway to what later became the Atlantic Hotel – plus a bathroom with a wave-making machine.

Trayles committed suicide in 1921, aged 76, 'suffering from an incurable gentleman's disease', and leaving the property to his housekeeper, Nancy Burrell.

1889

Frank James, brother to outlaw cowboy Jesse James and a member of his infamous gang, attended the 1889 Kentucky Derby where he saw Spokane win the race.

1890

Croydon racecourse closed.

1891

Every favourite won at Hamilton Park's two-day July fixture. During the same year, over in the States, every race in which he rode at a meeting in Chicago was won by jockey Monk Overton – to the distress of many attendant bookies. One such, known as The Ghost, took on the look of one, explained US racing historian Ed Hotaling, adding that for other layers, 'It was a near-death experience – some lost as much as $6,000.' It was estimated that Overton cost the bookies a 'combined, jaw-dropping $120,000'.

1891

'Betting is the manure to which the enormous crop of horseracing and race horse breeding in this and other countries is to a large extent due,' declared R. Black in his 1891 *The Jockey Club and its Founders*.

1892

Some 126 different racecourses staged national hunt races during this year, recorded Tony Lake in his excellent *Guide To Jump Racing 1892*, noting that the largest quantity at any one course was 79 at Lingfield, with Kempton next with 59. The most successful horses during the year were The Midshipmite, and The Saxon, both winning 12 races, but winner of the greatest amount of prize money was Father O'Flynn who won three times, collecting £1,761 in the process.

In Ireland in 1892 James 'Jemmie' Phelan was the most successful rider with 41 victories while the trainer of most of his rides, Larry Ryan topped that table with 37 wins worth £1,554.

1893

On 29 August a two-year-old horse called Domino won the Futurity Stakes at America's Sheepshead Bay course, collecting prize money of $49,000 and becoming, after just seven races, the highest-earning horse in the country, and surpassing Kingston, who was eight, as the highest earner in US racing history. Prize money was now increasing in leaps and bounds.

1894

Three races at Manchester all produced dead-heats, within the space of an hour, including Shancrotha and Red Ensign in the Manchester Cup.

Over in the USA, the now nine-year-old, Kingston retired with a record 89 wins and $138,917 prize money to his credit.

1894

Saratoga racecourse in the USA claimed to have 'the only race-track betting ring in America for women'.

1895

This year saw 128 courses in Britain staging 1,420 jumps races.

1895

Racegoers arriving to see the Kentucky Derby at Churchill Downs on 6 May were greeted by the sight of a brand new grandstand, topped by the famous Twin Spires.

1895

The *Racing Illustrated* edition of 4 December 1895, in its Turf Notes column, wrote, 'I fancy that W. Simms was the first coloured jockey to ride on an English racecourse. He brought a great reputation here from America and a victory in the first race in which he took part showed that he knew his business. None of our best performers could teach him anything in the art of getting well away; but his methods of riding differ very considerably from those of our best men. Like most American jockeys he seemed unable to keep his whip still for an instant. He has a great deal to learn before he can ride a clever and artistic finish according to our English ideas.'

Willie Simms brought a short-stirrup style of riding over to England. It had proved very effective in the States where he won five US 'Triple Crown' races and became a Hall of Fame jockey. En route to winning the US riding title in 1893 and 1894, Simms won back-to-back Belmont Stakes.

1896

The death was announced of Baron Maurice de Hirsch, born in Munich 63 years earlier, a popular racing owner who combined his enthusiasm for the turf with generosity towards those less fortunate than himself. He 'achieved a position and a fortune in the world of finance that has fallen to the lot of very few men', reported *Racing Illustrated*, revealing that 'none ever put their wealth to better use' and that he had been 'devoting all his winnings on the Turf to the London hospitals'. In 1892, which had been 'memorable for the exploits of his good mare, La Fleche' – who won the 1,000 Guineas and St Leger – he had 'handed over upwards of £33,000 for the good of the suffering poor'. According to inflation calculators, that £33,000 would equate to £4,467,512.41 today.

1896

An American magazine entitled *Turf, Field and Farm* ran a story in 1896, inviting readers to suggest ideas for the perfect race starting machine. It prompted one reader to outline his apparatus, 'An airship, suspended from which are a number of slings, which will be slipped around the bodies of the horses entered to race. When the bugle summons them to the post, the airship will sail to the paddock gate, receive the horses and float to the paddock gate. In order to prevent running away or fractiousness at the post, the horses are kept 18 inches above the ground. When everything is ready the starter touches a button, the slings release their hold, the horses drop to the ground, and off they go!'

Heath Robinson would have loved the idea and also an alternative suggestion which envisaged using a gigantic catapult to literally hurl the entire field of horses away from the starting post 'in the manner of a slingshot'. The author of the idea added, 'Of course, they will not strike the ground until several yards past the finish flag.'

1896

Why Not, foaled in 1881, finished fifth in the Grand National at the grand old age of 15 – his seventh National outing. He first contested it in 1889, finishing runner-up; in 1890 he fell and remounted to come fifth; he fell at the 29th in 1891; he missed the 1892 running; in 1893 he was back to finish third; won it in 1894 when he was 5-1 joint favourite; and was fifth in 1895. Arthur Nightingall, who rode him when he won and on several other occasions, said, 'He was such a game old chap, he struggled to the bitter end with unflinching resolution.' Why Not also won 23 other chases.

1896

In only the third running of America's 4m Maryland Hunt Cup over obstacles, Tom Whistler rode a horse called Kingsbury and they were going well until, related a witness, 'He streaked across the field, Whistler, all the while doing his best to pull him around. But Kingsbury had the bit in his teeth and couldn't be stopped. Heading straight for a barn, where he formerly had lived, the horse came to a dead stop at the door, tossing Whistler, bridle and all, over his head – and then trotted into his old stall to munch some oats.'

The race continued until, remembered Redmond Stewart, who finished fourth, 'As we neared the home stretch a big bay came thundering up from the rear and, to our amazement, it was Kingsbury. Whistler was bringing down his crop with each stride and the bay galloped past all of us to win the race. Later we learned that Whistler had rebridled and remounted Kingsbury in the barn, returned to the course and set out in pursuit.'

1896

The Derby was filmed for the first time and later shown at the Alhambra in London's Leicester Square.

1897

Manifesto won the Grand National at the third attempt, going off at 6-1 favourite. He missed the race in 1898, but landed a second triumph in 1889 under 12st 7lbs when 5-1 second-favourite. But he was almost prevented from so doing when, due to frosty ground, course workers spread hay on either side of some of the fences, including at the Canal Turn where, going well in the middle of the field, Manifesto jumped the fence well, but lost his footing on landing in the middle of the hay. His jockey, George Williamson, lost both stirrups and even touched the ground with his feet, but Manifesto somehow stayed upright and continued with rider intact. He would run in the race for an eighth and final time, finishing eighth in 1904, after which he was immediately retired aged 16.

1899

The moustachioed steeplechase specialist Frank Burns rode a winner on Opua, at the last meeting run at Thames Jockey Club, New Zealand, in late December. The jockey had another string to his bow – he was the Kiwi featherweight boxing champion for several years.

1900

Writer A.C. Blew, in his 1900 book *Racing*, made a prediction: 'Steeplechasing, once so popular a form of sport, now appears to have seen its best days. Now that cast-offs from Flat racing are put to jumping, and races are held over "made" courses with regulation fences, steeplechasing seems to have lost much of its popularity.'

1900

A starting gate was first used, at Lincoln racecourse.

1904

Northampton racecourse closed. From this year geldings were barred from running in the Derby.

1905

Foaled in 1905, Colin was one of four horses regarded as the very best American race horses of the first half of the 20th century, along with Syonsby, Man o'War and Citation. He was undefeated in 15 starts, though pressed to the limit when winning the 1908 Belmont Stakes. American Horse of the Year in 1907 and 1908, Colin proved subfertile at stud but managed to continue the male line of his grandsire, Domino.

1905

Licensing of UK trainers began.

1905

Still an apprentice, Elijah Wheatley became champion jockey with 124 winners.

1907

At the sprightly age of 17, the equine winner for the past two years of the Maryland Hunt Cup in the States, Garry Owen, completed his hat-trick.

1907

Bill Evans rode Apologue to win the Melbourne Cup, but the effort of getting down to the riding weight of 7st 9lb took its toll on the jockey who, reported the *Brisbane Courier*, 'was seen to stagger and fall in a dead faint' after the race. The newspaper added, 'the officials lifted him on to the scale, and he was weighed in an unconscious state, amidst intense excitement.'

1908

Actor Edward Underdown was born in this year. He later died in 1989 aged 81. He appeared alongside Humphrey Bogart in 1953 movie *Beat the Devil*, and also dead-heated with John Hislop as 1938's leading Flat racing amateur rider.

1909

Minoru, Derby winner this year, was exported to Russia only to be reportedly seized by Bolsheviks during the Revolution and executed for being an aristocrat.

1910

The horseracing phrase 'first past the post' is believed to have been used for the first time in the *Daily Post* newspaper from Hobart, Tasmania, on Thursday, 16 June 1910 – which was reporting the death of King Edward VII, who had died on 6 May, to be succeeded by George V: 'In connection with the death of the King, a singular coincidence has been noted. On Friday afternoon his Majesty's horse, Witch of the Air, won the Kempton Spring Plate at a moment when its Royal owner lay on the brink of death in London. As events turned out, his Majesty had raced successfully on his dying day. Witch of the Air carried King Edward's colours for the first time past the post early in the day and, as his Majesty did not lose consciousness until many hours later, he heard that the popular purple and gold had been carried to victory amid ringing cheers.'

1911

An interesting meeting at Perth where jockey Joe Kay rode five winners from five rides for trainer George Menzies, while the other race was voided after none of the three runners could complete the course.

1912

Pan Zareta began a six-year career, during which she ran at 24 different racecourses in Mexico, Canada and eight US states. She did once set a course record over a mile but was at her best over six furlongs or less. Eventually she won a record number of races – 76 in all, more than any other mare in US racing history, albeit most of them at a modest level. She was placed in the first three in another 52 races. She died of pneumonia while based at Fair Grounds racecourse and was buried there.

1912

The last 4f race run under Jockey Club rules took place on 27 May with Tossan winning.

1912

The grey filly, Tagalie, became the first of her sex to win both the 1,000 Guineas, at 20-1, and the Derby, at 100-8, in the same season. She was ridden by Kiwi jockey Les Hewitt in the former, and American Johnny Reiff in the latter. As if this wasn't enough for one season, two days later she was racing again, under a third jockey, George Stern, in the Oaks, as 1-2 favourite, but could only manage seventh. She was also unplaced in the St Leger.

1913

Read the record books, and you'll see that Louvois won the 1913 2,000 Guineas, and that Camballo was its winner in 1875.

But were these two Classic winners actually beaten in their races? Some believe they were.

William Allison was at Newmarket for 7-2 favourite Camballo's race, and he wrote in the authoritative *Bloodstock Breeders' Review*, 'Camballo was the first Two Thousand Guineas winner I ever saw, and I am quite sure he did not win it [33-1 chance], Claremont being the easy winner, on the far side of the course, right under the judge's box, which used to be on that side.

'All the rest of the field finished on the stand side, with Camballo in front, but the judge never saw Claremont. I am quite sure of this, because I was on the far side of the course, on the hill, from which one can see over the judge's box, and I know that Claremont won, as also – from the fact he was unplaced – that the judge never saw him.'

And another witness account in the article declared, 'Many of us are quite sure that [3-1 favourite] Craganour – who also finished right under the judge's box – and not Louvois [a 25-1 shot] won the 2,000 Guineas in 1913.'

1913

Trainer Arthur Yates, who rode some 460 winners as a jockey, also made an impression when in a race at Croydon he fell at the water jump, only to catch his horse's tail and leap back into the saddle over the quarters. The feat inspired a rhyme: 'In racing reports it is oft-times said, a jockey has cleverly won by a head. But Yates has performed, when all other arts fail, A more wonderful feat, for he won by a tail.'

He retired as a trainer in 1913 with getting on for 3,000 winners in that discipline, including 9-2 favourite Cloister in the 1893 Grand National, sent from his stables where he also had a menagerie of zebras, deer and rare birds.

1914

Jockey Bernard Dillon, who rode Lemberg to win the 1910 Derby, married legendary music-hall star Marie Lloyd in 1914, becoming her third husband. It didn't go well and, reportedly by now a regular drunkard, he appeared in court accused of beating her. They separated in 1920.

1914

Harpenden racecourse closed.

1915

Lady Nelson became the first female owner of a Grand National winner, as her Ally Sloper won at 100-8. In the same year, Patrobas – owned by Edith Widdis, who received the horse as a birthday present from her husband – became the first horse trained by a woman to win the Melbourne Cup. After being beaten in a two-horse race at the now defunct Rosedale Racecourse, Patrobas was sent to Charlie Wheeler, a top trainer of the day. Bobby Lewis became the first jockey to ride four Melbourne Cup winners. Patrobas carried rose pink silks and saddle cloth number 19.

1915

An anti-betting crusade had brought racing to a standstill in many American states, but it was returning, and did so in New Orleans on 1 January 1915. However, betting was now subject to 'severe restrictions', etheined the *New Orleans Times Picayune*. 'After paying $1.50 admission, the first procedure necessary to make a bet is to purchase a numbered badge for $1, which entitles the holder to enter the Palm Garden and paddock.

'Those desiring to make a bet walk up to the small tables at which are seated official stakeholders, about whom are gathered the men who will bet. When a bet is made – say $2 on Lady Moon at 2-1 to win, and her number on the program is number one in the first race – the man who takes the odds places his $2 on the table and it is covered by the $4 by the man laying the odds. The $6 is then picked up by the official stakeholder and placed in an envelope.

'The official stakeholder then writes on the outside of the envelope the number of the race, the number of the horse on the program, the position the horse is bet to finish and the number of the badge of the man accepting the odds.

'After the race the individual winning the bet goes to the official stakeholder, who wears a blue cap with a number on it, and shows him the number of his badge.

'The stakeholder then goes through the pile of envelopes until he comes to the number corresponding with the winner's badge number, and the envelope is handed over to him.'

1916

As the First World War progressed and some racing continued, those attending were looked upon with some suspicion in places. It was already the case that 'compulsory service having been established no one could be present at a race meeting unless on leave, exempted from service, or physically unfit'.

Lt. Col. Allen Cheshire, chief constable of Cambridgeshire and Huntingdonshire, took it on himself to make some checks, reporting in September, 'It may interest the general public to know that yesterday, a very close examination of all persons of apparently military age was made at Newmarket racecourse, with the result that no shirkers were discovered. The persons examined took it all in good part, petrol licences were inspected by the police and found in order, and no motor char-a-bancs arrived at the course.'

1917

Leading British equine artist Juliet McLeod, who was born in 1917, made it her business to chronicle the winner of every Classic race from 1947 onwards. Said *Sporting Life* of her, 'She ranks among the leading horse-painters of the day. Her repute is due in great part to the meticulous care with which she depicts her subjects; she will not glorify a horse – any anatomical defect it may have will appear in the finished painting.'

Charlotte Mullins of *Country Life* wrote, 'McLeod painted some of the greatest winners of the 1950s, 1960s and 1970s. As [George] Stubbs did, she tried to capture the character of each horse she painted, as well as its anatomical likeness.'

McLeod died in 1982. Trainer Mick Channon has one of her paintings on the wall of his owners' lounge, depicting Pneumatic, a horse bought by trainer Bill Wightman as a yearling for 65gns in 1952, and who went on to win 17 races, living at Wightman's Hampshire farm until his death, aged 30.

'The painting represents so much,' said Channon, 'It looks like something Stubbs could have done. Bill gave it to me at his 90th birthday party, and the note that accompanied it meant almost as much as the gift itself.

'Bill was the man I turned to when I bought my first horse, Cathy Jane, and he trained her with great success. He was old-fashioned but generous with his time and something of a father figure to me. He insisted patience was required for training horses – a belief he quickly forgot when I became HIS trainer!'

1918

Lady Jane Douglas became the first female owner to win the Derby, as Gainsborough won, with the race run at Newmarket.

1918

Born on 3 March 1918, legendary commentator Sir Peter O'Sullevan later noted that his 'most fortuitous racing experience' was 'contracting pneumonia on the eve of my intended association with an equally unskilled partner in wartime novice chase at Plumpton'.

1919

Racing writer T.H. Browne showed the effect of the First World War on racing by reporting, 'In 1913, 4,055 horses of various ages were saddled, and amongst these, prize money of £573,487 was distributed. The corresponding figures in 1918 were: horses 2,196;

prize money, £215,525.' But in 1919, 3,273 horses raced for prize money of £594,635, which compared favourably to 1913, which had been 'the most prosperous year the Turf had ever known'.

1920

An Australian colt foaled in 1920 was named after an obscure species of bird, but after 39 winless races – including two Melbourne Cups – his name started to become hijacked and used as slang for anything perceived as useless and slow. But at least Drongo's name lived on.

1921

The only horse to make it round in the Grand National without falling was winner Shaun Spadah, 100-9, owned by Sir Malcolm McAlpine, who came close to landing the spring double as his Senhora was runner-up in the Lincoln.

1921

The racecourse judge at Perth, racing historian Major Jack Fairfax-Blakeborough, confirmed the result of the Mansfield Chase, hoisting the numbers into the frame as the runners passed the post – only to realise the runners were racing on, and did so for another mile, resulting in another result being hoisted up to replace the initial one.

It transpired that the race card had, through a printing error, listed the race as being over 2m, but it was actually a 3m contest. The winner was White Swan, ridden by Billy Watkinson, who would win the 1926 Grand National on Jack Horner but die from a fall at Bogside three weeks later.

1921

Rosa Louisa Burnley, from Aylmerton in Norfolk, became the first woman to own a Cesarewitch winner as her unfancied 40-1 shot Yutoi, partnered by Henri Jelliss and trained by Lord George Dundas, romped home by four lengths in the 17-runner race, footage of which can still be viewed online. She had plenty of time to enjoy the success as she lived until January 1961, when she had reached the age of 100 and two weeks.

1922

Lord Airlie rode his own horse Master Robert to win Perth's Scottish Military Plate Chase, and unsurprisingly went off 5-1 outsider of three, with the rider putting up an astonishing 37lb overweight, taking the horse's weight to carry up to 13st 13lb.

However, the favourite pulled up lame and the other runner fell. Master Robert clearly welcomed carrying just 10st 5lb when he won a decent race two years later – the Grand National.

1922

Born in 1841, amateur jockey and trainer Arthur Yates died on 20 May 1922 after an eventful career, which saw him ride 460 winners, and train 2,590 of them. In 1872 he narrowly missed out on winning the Grand National – in which he rode four times – which he looked sure to do on Harvester, only for the horse to land awkwardly at the second-last and go lame. During that season he rode 67 winners, including 13 abroad. Two incidents illustrate the man's character – riding at Baden-Baden in Germany he fell, breaking his collarbone, but remounted and rode on, with the now non-working arm tucked in to his jacket, ending up beaten by a neck. Then, riding closer to home at Croydon, he took a fall at the water jump but, determined not to give up, managed to catch his horse Harold by the tail, with the aid of which he was able to remount and win the race.

Determined to continue riding, now into his 40s he was finally persuaded to give up after winning at Kempton in December 1884 when a female friend noted his increasing size, 'Well done, Arthur – but the joint is rather too big for the dish, now.'

In 1893 he managed to win the National as a trainer, with 9-2 favourite Cloister who, despite carrying 12st 7lb, set a course record.

1923

Tim Healy, governor of the Irish Free State, was delighted to be able to congratulate jockey Harry Beasley on riding his Pride of Arras to win a maiden plate at Punchestown – at the youthful age of 72. Harry was recorded riding in a Baldoyle race at the age of 83. He died in February 1939, aged 89.

1923

Spectators watching the 2,000 Guineas were left trying to work out whether they had seen the same race as the judge. Racing writer T.H. Browne reflected, 'In some respects it was a curious race; many onlookers were convinced that Knockando had won outright, but the judge gave the race to Ellangowan by a head, and allotted third place to D'Orsay. As a matter of fact the judge originally placed Legality second, ignoring Knockando completely, and it was a long time before the matter was put right. That an error had been committed there was, however, never a doubt, for Legality, being a grey horse, had been clearly observed coming in lengths behind the leaders. It is difficult to understand how such a mistake came to be made, but it may have arisen owing to the judge having mistaken Lord Woolavington's colours for those of Lord Furness.' The winner was bred by Lord Rosebery – his third win with a colt of his own breeding, Ladas in 1894 and Neil Gow in 1910 being the others.

1923

Saddle cloths were introduced.

1924

Sansovino, at 9-2 favourite, won the 27-runner Derby – the first winner of the race for, appropriately enough, the 17th Earl of Derby, who both owned and bred him, the first such for a member of the family of which he was now the head, since the 12th Earl of Derby had won it in 1787 with Sir Peter Teazle.

1925

When Hialeah racecourse in Florida opened for business in 1925, it devised a smart plan to get round the fact that gambling was illegal. Picture postcards of runners in each race were sold to punters fancying that horse – then the winning ones were purchased back at an appropriate premium.

1926

The 1926 Cheltenham Gold Cup – the third to take place – was presented to winning owner Frank Barbour after the victory of his steeplechaser, Koko, who won at 10-1 under Alfred Bickley, ridden by Tim Hamey. The 15ct, 40cm gold trophy cup and cover, standing 15.75in high, was by Edward Barnard & Sons Ltd. from London, made in 1925, its marble base set with a gold plaque inscribed 'THE CHELTENHAM GOLD CUP, WON BY, MR FRANK BARBOUR'S "KOKO", 9th MARCH 1926'. In November 2014, the trophy came up for sale at Graham Budd Auctions, sold with two laminated sheets of newspaper obituaries for the noted sportsman Mr Barbour – attracting a highest bid of £18,000.

Frank Barbour was a member of a famous Ulster family of linen makers and a keen sportsman, who had a training establishment in County Meath, complete with replicas of several famous fences, including some at Aintree. Somewhat eccentric, albeit fabulously wealthy he once fell during a point-to-point race, and still in his racing togs reportedly hitched a lift to Dublin and caught a ship to America. As one might!

1926

The BBC tried, unsuccessfully, to broadcast the Derby.

1926

A general strike adversely affected racing. It began the week after the Newbury First Spring Meeting. The Chester meeting, with the exception of the first day, was ruined, with few runners on day two and the day three card abandoned. For the next 16 days racing was at a standstill.

Lord Astor's Swift And Sure finished fourth in the 2,000 Guineas, a length and a half behind winner Colorado, but was 'badly interfered with by a dog which ran out on to the course,' according to a witness.

1927

Having been a guest at the annual Derby Luncheon, held at the London Press Club, the secretary for state for India, Lord Birkenhead, revealed that the Shah of Persia, asked whether he would like to see the Derby, had said, 'I am very conscious one horse must win, and I do not care which.' Lord Birkenhead added of the luncheon, 'As a tip-giving entertainment this has been one of the most ghastly failures in which I have ever taken part. We have heard a lot of nonsense about everyone wanting the best horse to win. They do not want the best horse to win. They want their own horse to win. They do not care a brass farthing whether it is the best or the worst – neither do I.'

1927

Sprig, the 8-1 favourite, won the 1927 Grand National, becoming the first winner of the great race owned by a woman, Mary Partridge. Her son had bred Sprig but he was killed during the First World War, serving with the Shropshire Yeomanry in 1918, so his mother put the horse in training, hoping to achieve his ambition of winning the National.

1928

Members – I use the word advisedly – of the Thoroughbred Breeders' Association's Annual General Meeting must have listened in stunned silence as they were addressed by Mr G.H. Drummond. For he was explaining that a 28-year-old stallion, Rabelais, standing at Maisons-Laffitte in France, had been sent to Professor Voronoff in order to undergo a possibly revolutionary operation, designed to extend his breeding career.

The illustrious professor had acquired another horse, which was 'perfectly useless for racing and of no value as a stallion'. This animal would be used as the donor for an operation during which 'parts of this animal's reproductive were grafted on to Rabelais'.

The bizarre, one might say Frankensteinese, operation had apparently initially proved successful. However, ostensibly from the effects of chloroform during the operation, Rabelais died several days later.

The AGM was told a similar operation had been performed in Germany, but had also proved fatal for the recipient.

Members were then asked to vote on a motion moved by George Lambton 'that this association strongly disapproves of the practice of gland grafting'. It was carried unanimously.

1928

For the first time, a horse bred and owned by a reigning monarch won a Classic race, when King Edward VII's Scuttle landed the 1,000 Guineas.

1929

The Grand National had a record field of 66 runners.

1929

The *Bloodstock Breeders' Review* of 1929 described the betting system at the races in Tokyo, Japan, where, 'A day's racing begins at nine in the morning and ends at dusk. There are 11 events on the card. A penalty is carried for every race won and after winning 15 times a horse must be retired. No horse over six years old is allowed to race. Betting is conducted with a totalisator. No one may have more than one bet on a race and that bet must be one of £2. When an outsider wins his backers are paid no more than £20 – 9-1. The surplus going to the race club.'

1929

Has much changed since the 1929 edition of the *Bloodstock Breeders' Review* pointed out, 'It is notorious that racing in Great Britain has for more than a generation been a ruinously expensive pastime, and the marvel is that the public have tolerated the excessive charges they were called upon to pay'?

1929

A totalisator was used for the first time, on 2 July at Newmarket and Carlisle.

1930

Bloodstock Breeders' Review ran a small article concerning, 'John Faulkner, who achieved a reputation as a jockey over 70 years ago, and celebrated in March the 102nd anniversary of his birth at Appleford, Berkshire. As a youth he rode at 4st 7lb, and it is on record that after his first race at Epsom he received 3d as his riding fee. He rode at Abingdon Steeplechases when he was in his 75th year. Married twice, he is the father of 32 children.'

1930

Members of the Jockey Club were asked by the stewards to pass a rule that 'no horse shall run unnamed'. The motion, which would have affected only two-year-olds as older horses were already banned from running unnamed, was bizarrely rejected on the reported grounds that 'as there is not an unlimited supply of good and appropriate names, it is a pity to waste them on horses that disappear from the Turf before they are three years old'. It was also decided that in future dead-heats would no longer be run off.

During this year, two trainers were warned off by the stewards for doping runners.

1931

Owner Mr H.F. Clayton fancied the chances of his two horses landing the Autumn Double of the Cambridgeshire and the Cesarewitch. William Hill didn't fancy his chances, and offered him 1,000-1 against it happening. Clayton, a Yorkshireman from Huddersfield, thought that was a very fair offer and staked £100. Clayton's Disarmament duly won the Cambridgeshire, at 18-1, and the double was on. He had Sixwheeler going for him in the 24-runner Cesarewitch – and, as any serious punter will by now probably have guessed, it finished second!

Amazingly, despite that huge liability with Hill, Sixwheeler went off at a starting price of 100-1, just over a length behind 100-6 winner Noble Star.

1931

For the first time the Kentucky Derby was broadcast live to the UK and heard on the BBC.

1931

A three-horse race at Pungarehu Racing Club in New Zealand's 1931 meeting didn't exactly set the blood of those present flowing strongly – the Farmer's Plate over a mile and a quarter saw Te

Poka finish first with just one betting ticket staked on him, while runner-up Ranso had attracted not a single wager, and The Washer in third had an absolute flood of five tickets staked on him. A protest saw Te Poka disqualified for being ineligible to start, so the unbacked Ranso was declared the winner.

1932

Born in 1875, although neither he nor anyone else knew precisely when, Edgar Wallace grew up to become a hugely popular writer of thrillers, film scripts and mystery novels, making a fortune along the way – some of which he began to use towards his move into racing journalism, ownership and betting. As the 1932 *Bloodstock Breeders' Review* said in its obituary, 'When his purse began to wax fat he set sail on the perilous sea of ownership, and later joined the ranks of breeders. Betting became one of his foibles. These adventures proved ruinous. Shortly after his death an examination of his financial affairs revealed a deficit no less than £60,000. His widow attributed this seemingly incredible state of things to losses due to his association with racing.'

1933

Tote straight forecast bets were introduced – but were only available on races of three or four runners, as they were designed to be a substitute for place betting, not permitted in such small fields.

1934

Uniquely, Brown Jack won a Champion Hurdle, and six consecutive runnings of Royal Ascot's Queen Alexandra Stakes, from 1929-34. He also won the Goodwood, Doncaster and Chester Cups and an Ebor Handicap. He had a pub and a train named after him. He was retired in the winner's circle at Ascot. Not content with his immortal achievements on the racecourse, Brown Jack reportedly began haunting the Mill Ride Golf Club near Ascot, whose managing director Dickie Freemantle explained in late 1993: 'Brown Jack was buried under the 170-acre estate. The master greenkeeper has seen a phantom horse twice while setting off the sprinklers at night.' Other golfers have reported hearing 'neighing and galloping sounds.' Others have apparently been 'mysteriously knocked over' on the greens.

1934

After winning the Lancarty Chase at Perth on Noir et Rouge, the amateur jockey Peter Payne-Gallwey was packed off to Egypt with his regiment, the 11th Hussars. During the Second World War, Payne-Gallwey captured a German general behind enemy lines, in a mobile brothel. Really. He won the Distinguished Service Order and two bars.

1935
Some 49 two-year-olds ran in the Beckhampton at Newbury.

1936
The horse Victor Norman won the Champion Hurdle at 4-1 in 1936. He was trained by American amateur rider and trainer Morgan de Witt Blair, whose nickname was 'Bam', allegedly as a result of his habit of exclaiming 'Bam!' as he entered the weighing room, and/or on injecting himself prior to going out and riding in races. That he might need something in his system to counter potential pain was illustrated by his antics in the 1921 Grand National in which he partnered Bonnie Charlie – a combination which proceeded to fall at the fourth. But Bam remounted, and fell again. On the sequence continued, and eventually they were hopelessly adrift and Bam had broken his collarbone, so they called it a day. Apparently he had bet that he would get round.

Four years later he was again taking part in the National, this time on Jack Horner, having sweated off 18lb in 48 hours to make the weight and sporting a livid scar as a result of an appendix operation a mere two weeks earlier. Somehow Bam got round in seventh place, probably winning another wager on so doing.

1937
Owner-breeder and later trainer Florence Nagle went close to a unique double as one of her Irish wolfhounds was declared the Supreme Champion at Crufts, but her 100-1 shot Sandsprite was beaten into second place in the Derby by Mid-day Sun, after which she commented, 'Not bad for a horse which one newspaper said was only good enough to give rides at the seaside.' Florence led the fight for women's right to hold training licences, taking on the Jockey Club virtually single-handedly and winning her case. She died in 1988, aged 94.

1937
The two main stands at Cardiff's Ely racecourse were 'totally destroyed in a fire', recorded Brian Lee in his *History of Cardiff Racecourse*. 'One Saturday morning in March 1937, two night nurses at Ely Lodge Hospital, which was situated right behind the stands, saw flames shooting up from the roof of Tattersalls.

When the Cardiff City Fire Brigade arrived on the scene the whole stand was blazing furiously from end to end. In little over an hour both stands were reduced to smouldering ruins.'

There were efforts to save racing at the course and this year's Easter Meeting went ahead with temporary wooden stands being constructed. Reportedly 300 horses were entered.

However, this was the beginning of the end for the course, and on 27 April 1939, Grasshopper, ridden by Keith Piggott, won the Club Juvenile Handicap Hurdle, the last event of the meeting – and the final one to be run at the course.

1938

Catalogue was the first horse trained by a woman to win the Melbourne Cup – but her name was not permitted to appear in the record books as Australia did not recognise female trainers in 1938, so the official credit was given to Allan William McDonald, who was given a temporary licence to get round the rules, rather than his wife Granny McDonald

1938

The first live television broadcast of the Derby.

1939

A horse called Starlet had run 'shockingly' in two previous starts in Hong Kong, so badly that only three $5 tickets on her were sold by the tote. But not only did the horse win, she returned extraordinary odds of 7,500-1, paying each of the three ticket holders $3,770.60.

1940

Trainer Alfred Day, born in 1874, died. He sent out Royal Lancer to win the 1922 St Leger – always stylishly turned-out in appearance, he acquired the nickname 'Flash Alf' during his time based in Newmarket.

1941

After the Japanese occupied Hong Kong during the Second World War, explained the book *The Royal Hong Kong Jockey Club*, 'Horses were in such short supply that programmes were supplemented by races for wooden horses, made of three-ply, 15 and a half inches long and 8 and a half inches high. They "galloped" down a contraption of wires in front of the grandstand. Winners were penalised by having weights removed so they would slide down the wires more slowly.'

1942

Adelaide-based jockey K. Parris was disqualified for six months after being found guilty of hanging on to the tail of a rival runner – just as it was about to take a fence during a steeplechase.

1943

Racing continued in the USA during the war but there was a shortage of male steeplechase riders, so Judy Johnson was granted a licence by the Maryland Racing Commission, riding at Pimlico and becoming the first female jockey in sanctioned steeplechases in the States – and she also rode in Canada, scoring seven winners there before concentrating on becoming a trainer.

1944

Jockey John 'Skeets' Martin died in March of this year after an eventful racing career. Plenty of jockeys have been described as being ice-cold in a finish – but this American took that ability somewhat farther, as he not only rode winners on the snow at St Moritz in his day, but also excelled in tobogganing on the Cresta Run, and was no mean performer on the curling rink there.

Born on 25 January 1875 near Pennsylvania, his family moved to Santa Clara where Martin, then 15, became an apprentice rider.

His riding career suffered a setback when, despite already having the best part of 300 winners on the scoresheet, rumours began that he was not averse to the occasional pre-ordained outcome of a race.

So, as the 20th century loomed, Skeets headed for England, quickly notching up some 50 winners at a one-in-three ratio.

A two-month suspension for rough riding resulted in the Jockey Club declining his permit to ride in the UK, so he moved to Germany before returning to England in 1902, promptly winning the Derby on Ard Patrick, then suffering a collarbone injury which resulted in a lengthy stint out of action.

In 1903 he returned to win the 2,000 Guineas on Rock Sand. In 1909 Martin rode St Martin, well fancied for the Derby, but they fell. For the next few years he continued to ride his fair share of winners – despite a 1914 tobogganing injury.

Early in the First World War, Martin and his wife Florence left their home in Newmarket and moved to California, returning to the UK in 1916. He was the second-leading jockey in Britain in 1917, with 32 winners.

Martin now had homes in Newmarket, California and St Moritz. He was still an active participant in winter sports in Switzerland and participated in winter horseracing in St. Moritz.

But Martin fell on hard times during retirement in the late 1930s and 1940s, as a result of unwise investments.

Destitute, he died in March 1944 at a nursing home in Switzerland. His funeral was reportedly attended by only three mourners.

1945

Elizabeth Graham became the first woman in the history of the American turf to exceed half a million dollars in earnings by her stable of runners in a single season, in 1945. Her runners collected $593,670 in prize money, marginally short of the outright world record established the previous year by Warren Wright's Calumet stable.

1945

The war had a significant impact on racing and racecourses – for instance, racing continued at Newbury early on but the final meeting there was on 20 September 1941 before, following the Dunkirk evacuations, the course was handed over to the US forces as a marshalling yard, with petrol and stores for the North African landings assembled and despatched from there. Subsequently, enormous quantities of engineering equipment, bridging material and invasion stores were concentrated there prior to the main assault on Europe.

The course was used successively as a military camp, a main supply depot and a vast marshalling yard and storage dump. Fixtures were only resumed in 1949.

At the outbreak of hostilities the majority of UK racecourses were requisitioned by the services. Yarmouth racecourse sustained heavy damage by high explosives and incendiary bombs, while scientific experiments with smoke barrages contributed to its problems, along with a huge anti-tank ditch, one of the widest and deepest in the country.

Kempton Park was used as a prisoner-of-war camp, and before it could be used again for racing 500 tons of concrete had to be removed from the Jubilee course. The whole area abounded with barbed wire and the parade ring had become 'one vast bed of rhubarb,' according to a contemporary report, which added, 'Fittings on the racecourse buildings completely disappeared – even to the mechanism of the clocks on the stands and jockeys' number board – while stables sustained bomb blast damage.'

Sandown Park was not as badly affected, as Units of the Brigade of Guards occupied the course – with the War Office reportedly paying the course some £10,000 per year.

Epsom was damaged by flying bombs, while Goodwood managed to fend off efforts by the War Office to requisition the course itself, after they had occupied the tote and some other outbuildings. The course did come under threat from an unexpected source when, in autumn 1947, the track was infested by a plague of leatherjackets, whose grubs destroyed the roots of the downland turf, causing bald patches to appear.

Leicester was taken over by the army, with stables and tote buildings used as sleeping quarters – but two 1940 meetings actually took place there while the army was in residence.

Wolverhampton became headquarters of a rocket battery, while Wincanton's course had stakes driven into the ground to prevent enemy aircraft landing, leaving the track almost derelict by the end of hostilities.

At Sedgefield they had breathed a sigh of relief when the army moved out – only for squatters to move in, taking possession of the racecourse buildings, despite not a single door, and only a few windows, still remaining in place. Racing on Boxing Day 1946 was unable to go ahead when the squatters remained in residence.

Neither Derby nor Gatwick returned to action after the war was over.

Journalist Abingdon Bottom wrote in 1949, 'The debit side is far outweighed by the magnificent manner in which Britain's racecourses – many war-torn almost beyond recognition – have undergone Cinderella-like transformations to resume playing their part in the racing world.

Minor miracles of improvisation have been performed by executives who, limited by licence in the amount of reconstruction permissible, have used unrationed and surplus materials to bring their savaged courses up to the required standards.

'And racegoers who may complain a little at the poor, or lack of, amenities at some of the re-born tracks should think again before becoming too bitter in their denunciation of the powers-that-be.'

1946–47

A history of racing organised by the Tasmanian Turf Club from 1814 onwards, *From Then…Till Now*, by W.C.S. Oliver recalled that during the mid-1940s, 'A nice gesture by the committee was a meeting to help the Food For Britain Appeal – a substantial sum was raised. Parcels were bought and sent to the secretary of the Jockey Club for distribution to British jockeys, trainers and others who were in need.'

1947

A £6 wager threatened the very fabric of bookmaker William Hill's business in 1947. Explained probably the greatest bookmaker of all, 'The bet I shall always remember above all else was the case of a "dour Scotsman" who invested a £6 win double on Jockey Treble in the Lincoln of 1947, and Double Sam in the Grand National of the same year. The price I laid him was 50,000-1 [a potential liability of £300,000] and when Mr S. Oxenham's five-year-old came storming through his field to win the Lincoln [at 100-1] literally "on the post" we, who make our living at racing, had one more example of a small betting man apparently knowing more than we do.

'Now, at this time, ten minutes past three on that Wednesday afternoon, Double Sam was a 500-1 chance for the Grand National, but immediately became one of our "bogeys".

'I therefore instructed one of my staff to approach the "dour Scotsman" and see whether he would be interested in hedging part of his wager, to ensure his being on a winner no matter what the result of the National, and also to reduce our liability.

'This small punter was an exceedingly clever businessman and after much persuasion, in which I personally took a hand, he agreed to lay us £150,000 to £1,500 Double Sam, thereby reducing our liability by half and ensuring his winning at least £1,494, even if his second nomination should not be the winner.

'Double Sam met his doom at the 28th fence and our client, although backing a losing double, had still won £1,494 for a £6 investment.'

That double, had it come off, would have cost Hill the 2022 equivalent of £3,752,100.

1947

On 22 February 1947 the Royal Calcutta Turf Club celebrated its 100th anniversary. Racing is known to have been taking place in Calcutta as early as 1769.

1947

Complaints were made by Newmarket trainers in October, 'The walking strips encircling the Heaths have had the appearance of prairie fires when strings of horses travel along them. A chalky dust, several inches deep, rises and smothers both horses and riders. It is a pity the Jockey Club cannot afford a few more water carts for use during periods of drought. All sorts of insects and flies accumulate in this dust, it is an opinion that most of the heel-bug and a lot of the dry summer cough originates in this filth.'

1947

Following the war, racing was under way again in Germany by this year – with Munich and Frankfurt in the American Zone; Hassloch, Baden-Baden and seven other Rhineland locations in the French; Cologne in the British; and Dresden, Leipzig and Berlin in the Soviet Zone. Many grandstands were destroyed by bombing and tracks ploughed up while horses became scattered throughout Europe.

1948

With two to jump in the 1948 Grand National, 100-1 outsider Zahia was challenging for the lead under jockey Eddie Reavey, and owner N.F. Gee was looking sure to cash in on his bet of £100 each way at odds of 100-1 until, inexplicably, Reavey and Zahia took the wrong course, missing out the final fence, and being instantly disqualified. Reavey, it transpired, had walked the course and mistakenly thought that the Chair and Water Jump should be bypassed on their left, not their right, on the final circuit. Thus, in running, he took a path towards the Chair omitting the 30th. The 50-1 shot, Sheila's Cottage, took advantage to win, but showed scant gratitude to jockey Arthur Thompson – when he visited her after the race, she bit off the top of his finger.

1948

On 8 March, top-flight jockey Al (Albert) Snider from Alberta, Canada, 46; Tobe Trotter, in his late 40s and a trainer at Hialeah, and their racing enthusiast friend Don Fraser, a member of the Ontario Jockey Club, were getting towards the end of the fishing trip in a small boat they had set out on with three other mutual friends in the Florida Keys.

They were reported missing after the six of them listened to a racing broadcast and then just Snider, Trotter and Fraser set out for a little more angling. They were spotted by people on another vessel at 6.27pm through binoculars – but two minutes later there was no sign of them. Weather conditions were reportedly perfectly acceptable. The boat had plenty of safety equipment on board.

Other reported details include that the sea was calm. The skiff was half a mile from land, and in shallow water no deeper than four feet. If the boat ran into trouble, they could easily have swum, or even waded, ashore.

The three were never seen again despite a thorough search by boats and coastguard planes. Several days later, reportedly on 13 March, their empty skiff was found on Rabbit Key with no evident damage, although its outboard motor and oars were missing.

A little more than a year later, *American Weekly* columnist Dan Parker ran a story claiming, 'Miami's underworld is whispering stories that Citation's jockey [Snider] met his death through gangland vengeance because he wouldn't obey the orders of a gambling syndicate.'

Snider rode Citation five times at the age of two and four times after turning three. He won all nine races, but after Snider's disappearance the horse became one of the all-time greats by landing the US Triple Crown.

However, few bought in to that theory, or to rumours of a Cuban connection. Snider's daughter Nancy spoke of being contacted by people claiming to have seen her father.

A barnacle-encrusted bottle was washed up on shore at Hallandale, Florida, four months after the disappearance. Inside was a note with a scribbled message, 'Help. One dead. No joke. Al S.' This was likely to have been a poor-taste hoax.

Another writer online asserted, 'I'm friends with an 80-something fellow who worked at Calumet during the Citation era, and who knew Snider personally. When I once asked him what he thought had happened to Snider, he instantly replied matter-of-factly, "Why, the gangsters got him. Everyone knew that."'

Nonetheless, problems as the result of a sudden storm remains the favoured explanation.

1949

He watched the first Kentucky Derby in 1875 as a 13-year-old from his father's grocery wagon flatbed, parked in the infield, and he carried on watching them until 1949. In 1902 he – Louisville tailor Matt J. Winn – had formed a syndicate of investors to take over the Churchill Downs racecourse where the Derby was run. He was credited with making the event one of the world's great races. He died, aged 88, on 6 October 1949.

1949

The Czechoslovak Jockey Club contacted the Austrian Jockey Club to inform them that the three-year-old filly from Czechoslovakia, Heda, who had won the 1948 Austrian Derby was, in fact, a four-year-old mare named Lyra.

1949

Mao Zedong, then leader of China's communist party, banned horseracing as 'an immoral pursuit'.

1950

One of very few trainers whose sons would go on to do likewise by winning a Melbourne Cup was Jim Cummings, responsible in 1950 for 25-1 winner Comic Court. His son Bart grew up to be a multiple winner of the race, while James Wilson, whose Briseis was the 1876 winner, sired son James junior to win in 1899 with Merriwee.

1951

Larry Wiggins, who was riding Akbar in the 1951 Melbourne Cup, had been promised the first prize money of £10,000 if he won on the 7-1 shot. He finished second by three quarters of a length behind 10-1 Delta, and was paid a losing fee of £6.

1952

It was reported that former champion boxer Randolph Turpin (better known as Randy Turpin, who in 1951 became world middleweight champion when he defeated the legendary Sugar Ray Robinson) was now a keen horse rider and racing man, with an ambition to win a steeplechase, and that Sir Gordon Richards had gifted him a whip to help him do so. In 2011, Peter Williams of Denbigh told Liverpool's *Daily Post* newspaper that Turpin had lived in Bodelwyddan, where: 'I can recall that he used to ride a horse up the High Street of Rhyl – if memory serves me right, it was a white horse.'

Another celebrity of the times, stage and radio star Charlie Chester, was another regular rider, who was about to become a race horse owner. He also owned a casino.

1954

Goodwood was the first British track to introduce a racecourse commentator to call the action during races. Not everyone was delighted – including Sir Peter O'Sullevan, who explained that as he was already calling races on the TV and radio, 'It was an intrusion on the fact that one could bet in running. I was one of only a handful who knew what was going on.'

1954

It was reported in May that readers of a London evening newspaper included Mrs Mirabel Topham (Mrs Grand National) and (wealthy, eccentric owner) Miss Dorothy Paget in a list of 'England's six worst-hatted women'.

1954

Two jockeys who had ridden Derby winners took part in a novice hurdle race at Wolverhampton on Boxing Day. They were Michael Beary (Midday Sun, Mid-day Sun, or Mid-Day Sun, in 1937, whose owner Mrs G.B. Miller became the first woman to lead in the winner in the race's history) and Lester Piggott (Never Say Die, 1954).

1955

Thundering Legion was backed from 33-1 to 7-2 to win in Adelaide, Australia, on 21 May of this year. The big gamble alerted steward Fred Everest, who discovered pre-race that jockey Bill Attrill was equipped with a battery-powered whip, designed to administer an electric shock to the horse at a crucial moment of the action.

Attrill was stood down, but a substitute jockey was allowed to ride the horse – who stormed to a legitimate victory.

Attrill, though, was disqualified for ten years, and trainer Noel Conway for life.

1956

Swaps had won the 1955 Kentucky Derby, and won eight of his nine races that season. He raced ten times, from California to Florida, winning eight of them and, in the process setting or equalling world-record times from one mile to one and five-eighths of a mile. The horse sustained two fractures of a cannon bone in October, endangering his life – and as a result, spent four months suspended in a sling in his stall, his legs barely resting lightly on the ground. He died in 1972 with career winnings of $848,900 to his name.

1956

Jockey Dave Dick completed a unique double, taking the Lincoln on Gloaming in 1941 and, fortuitously after Devon Loch collapsed on the run-in, adding the Grand National on E.S.B. in 1956. The Devon Loch mystery will never be solved but his trainer Peter Cazalet had suffered a couple of other National disasters – in 1936 his Davy Jones was ahead two out only for the reins to break in jockey Anthony Mildmay's hands, thus losing control of his mount, who ran out at the last, scattering spectators in the process. And in 1948 Mildmay was struck down by cramp on Cromwell, who had looked likely to win, but without full assistance from his rider could only finish third.

1958

In only his second public ride, Brian Lawrence won the Welsh Grand National on 20-1 outsider Oscar Wilde.

1959

On their way to the post at Ascot, on 26 September 1959, Priddy Fair whipped round, unseating jockey Manny Mercer and kicking him on the floor, fatally injuring the 29-year-old whose biggest success was probably a 100-1 victory on Jockey Treble in the 46-runner Lincolnshire Handicap in 1947.

1960

On his way to York in October 1960, one winner short of completing a seasonal total of 100 winners for the first time, jockey Joe Sime, who was driving alongside his wife, was forced to 'dawdle for some time behind a bus'. It wasn't just any bus: this one boasted the number plate GET 100 – and, as Joe's wife said later, 'When I saw that number on the Mexborough bus, not far from Tadcaster, I felt all wobbly inside. It was the most extraordinary coincidence.' Indeed it was, as Joe duly clocked up the ton on the well-named Go Man Go.

1961

For the first time, the first three home in the Derby were all owned by women, with third-placed 13-2 shot Pardao owned by C.O. Iselin; runner-up Dicta Drake, 100-8 was in the colours of Suzy Volterra and the dramatic winner, Psidium, an unconsidered 66-1 chance, came dramatically from last to first over the last half-mile under Roger Poincelet to land the £34,548 prize money for Arpad Plesch, wife of a millionaire banker.

1962

J.P. McManus, bookie, owner and punter, confessed his first bet was one shilling – 5p – each way on Orchardist, at 25-1, for the

1962 Cesarewitch. The horse duly passed the post in front, but was disqualified and placed second. McManus would have still made a profit, though.

1962

One of the top jump riders of his day before becoming a leading trainer, Fred Winter visited the USA in October, where he won the New York Turf Writers Cup at Belmont Park on Baby Prince.

1963

The last thing jockey Paddy Cowell expected to happen on 16 April was that he would end up that day riding the winner of the Welsh Grand National – particularly as he didn't even have a ride in the race. However, when Fred Winter injured his ribs in the first race, riding against Paddy, he had to pull out of riding Motel in the big race later that afternoon, and Paddy came in for the spare ride on the eventual 7-1 winner. Not only that, Paddy later gave Fred a lift home since he couldn't drive because of his injuries. Winter invited him in when they got back, and told him, 'You turn me over at the ditch, ride my horse to victory in the big race – and now you sit here drinking my whisky.'

1964

America's New Jersey Hunt Cup race attracted just two runners – and both refused at the fourth fence, the water jump. Acerado was finally persuaded to go on by rider Paddy Smithwick, but further problems at the water next time round meant they finally completed the course in a time of 20 minutes – compared with an average time of not much over six minutes. And to complete Smithwick's day, the stewards judged the event to be a no-race as a result of 'unauthorised assistance' being given at the water jump.

1965

The first race to be started from stalls in Britain was the Chesterfield Stakes at Newmarket on 8 July 1965. The winner, Track Spare, was trained by Ron Mason and ridden by Lester Piggott.

1966

The Tote Jackpot bet was introduced – and in October the Duchess of Norfolk won £2,795 from it for a 25p stake.

1967

Jockey Club and National Hunt handicapper from 1911, the grandly named Charles Windham Leycester Penrhyn-Hornby, died aged 92. He once wrote, 'I came to the conclusion that a handicapper should be stone-deaf, but very keen-sighted.'

1968

'Dark Jet is so far in front he can fall and still win,' declared Sandown's racecourse commentator in December 1968, just as Terry Biddlecombe's mount came down at the last, slithering along the ground on his belly with Biddlecombe somehow staying put, then galvanising the horse back into action and going on to win by five lengths.

1969

Winner of a race in Victoria, Australia, the horse Major Leon was drug tested in 1969 – after which it was revealed that the urine sample tested had proved to be 'of human origin'. Connections were fined for 'improper practices'.

1970

Leo O'Brien rode Augustus Bay to win the Bushwick Hurdle at Belmont Park – only to face an objection on the grounds of 'alleged interference' by the runner-up's jockey, Michael O'Brien – Leo's brother. The stewards decided the result should stand. Tragically, Michael was paralysed from the waist down as a result of a fall during the Carolina Cup in 1974, as the race was won by Leo on Breaking Dawn.

1971

The very droll writer Ogden Nash, who was born in 1902 and died in 1971, once observed accurately, 'The people who think they can wind up ahead of the races are ... everybody who has ever won a bet.'

1972

In his eternal quest for winners, Lester Piggott rode Sailing Home, trained by veteran Joyce Edgar Jones, to win the New Zealand International Invitation Stakes at Te Rapa, later described by Kiwi racing writer Jack Glengarry as 'the race of the decade' in that country.

1972

Brothers Barry and Peter Brogan rode a dead-heat in April at Perth in the Argaty Handicap Chase, possibly the first such occurrence.

1972

Aussie jockey Peter Morgan was stood down from his mounts at Victoria Park by stewards of the South Australian Jockey Club because his hair was too long.

In February 1953 another jockey named Peter Morgan came to a tragic end. Reported the *Cairns Post*, 'Prominent jockey Peter Morgan (37) was drowned today in a canal 50 yards from his home at Hendra.

'Morgan and trainer Merv Cavanagh swam across the canal without difficulty to see to the safety of a mare and foal. Swimming back through rapidly swelling waters they realised they could not make it and turned back to a log. Cavanagh struggled to the log and found that Morgan had disappeared. Morgan's body was found later.'

1973

Bookies were hammered hard as 11-10 Royal Mark won at Windsor in November 1973, on the day that Capt. Mark Phillips wed Princess Anne.

1974

The 100th running of the Kentucky Derby took place in the presence of Princess Margaret, who was involved in the trophy presentation.

1975

Until 1979, women were forbidden from competing against men in Australian horseracing. One woman, from North Queensland, decided at an early age that she couldn't let gender stop her becoming a jockey.

Wilhemena Smith – also called Bill 'Girlie' Smith – lived her life in the early 1900s as a man to pursue her dream.

Only after her death in 1975 was her secret revealed. She was buried in Herberton in an unmarked grave until Herberton Lions Club discovered her story and organised to put a tombstone on her grave, reading, 'In loving memory, Wilhemena "Bill" Smith, 1886 – 1975. Australia's first licensed female jockey.'

Ivan Searston edited a book, *Ghosts of a Mining Town*, providing the little detail known about Smith's extraordinary life: 'Simply put, she's an enigma. She carved out a life for herself and her life depended on her being male.'

For 70 years, Smith lived as a recluse in order to find employment easier and pursue her dreams. Orphaned at a young age, Smith, born in 1886, grew up in Western Australia. 'At 16 she decided she had enough, got on a ship and ended up in North Queensland,' Searston said.

'When she came into North Queensland was uncertain but she did some mining to the west of Cairns and, probably around her 30s, she became very interested in horses and became a licensed jockey and a licensed trainer.'

Under the alias of Bill Smith, she found success on the racetrack in the 1940s and 1950s, competing in Queensland towns such as Cairns, Mareeba, Mount Garnet, Innisfail and Herberton. 'At a regional level, she was fairly successful,' said Searston – himself a Herberton local.

1976

It was reported by writer Joe Hirsch in 1976, 'The New York Racing Association now wisely owns two canoes, because the steeplechase set invariably steals one on the eve of the Travers. It happened again Friday evening. The canoe was found on the roof of a barn.' Hirsch was referring to the fact that it had become a tradition at Saratoga, home of the long-established Travers Stakes, for jump jockeys to steal the canoe in the track's infield lake, traditionally painted in the colours of each year's winning owner's silks.

1976

Ruff's Guide to the Turf listed 14 'Winning women riders on the flat 1976', with Diana Bissill having the greatest number of rides (20) and of winners (five). Diana Weeden had 22 rides for three winners; Margaret Bell and Brooke Sanders both won two from, respectively 11 and seven races.

In the next year's edition, 19 winning women riders were listed, with Elain Mellor scoring eight victories from 24 rides, and her closest rival Franca Vittadini on six from 15.

1977

Martin Blackshaw – perhaps a journeyman jump jockey at home, although his journeys included many to Norway and Belgium where, in both, he became champion – was the 'peacock' of the jockeys' room, dressing more smartly for racing than many would for dinner at a high-class restaurant.

On one occasion he appeared wearing a pristine, three-piece white suit, not surprisingly producing wolf-whistles from his changing room colleagues. Fellow rider Ian Watkinson appeared, having earlier purchased a pot of 'invisible' ink from a joke shop and threw it over the spotless suit. Blackshaw's response was instant and violent and Wilkinson, tough guy though he was, ran for it. Fortunately for Wilkinson, the ink marks eventually vanished.

On Christmas Day 1977, Blackshaw was riding at Cagnes Sur Mer and scored an unusual double – winning the biggest race of the day and nabbing the best festive present as he popped the question and was able to announce his engagement to Cherry Dwyer.

1977

It was difficult to determine the biggest story to emerge from the Oaks. It was won by the Queen's filly, Dunfermline, a 6-1 chance ridden by Willie Carson and trained by Dick Hern. But pre-race, Lester Piggott's mount Durtal's saddle slipped in the parade ring. Startled, she began to run and Lester was thrown, but with a foot caught in a stirrup. He was dragged along until the horse crashed into a fence – but just before she did, the stirrup leather broke and Lester was freed. He was taken to hospital by ambulance but no serious damage was diagnosed.

The Queen, Willie Carson and Dunfermline landed a Royal Classic double later in the season when they won the St Leger, this time at even longer odds of 10-1.

And Lester's season got better, too, as he won the Prix de l'Arc de Triomphe on Alleged, returning marginally under 4-1, beaten when odds-on by Dunfermline in the St Leger, with a front-running masterclass for trainer Vincent O'Brien. And the horse returned in 1978 to complete an Arc double.

1978

Stetchworth reared and almost threw jockey Taffy Thomas at Redcar in September 1978. They recovered to win the race, but afterwards gunshot marks were found on the horse's rump – he had apparently been shot by youths hidden in nearby long grass.

1978

Paul Wright was headmaster at Slindon College in West Sussex. He came up with the novel idea of running a racing stables from the premises. At one point there were ten horses being stabled there, with pupils at the college playing a big part in looking after them, and in one instance, an 18-year-old student actually rode one in a hurdles race at Cartmel.

There was even a half-hour BBC TV film made about probably the only horses actually trained on school premises.

The stables still exist at the college today, but they are no longer inhabited by race horses.

1979

The opening race on a Worcester card in October 1979 was to all intents and purposes unexceptional, apart from the outcome with 33-1 Quantock Mauger winning. However, a stewards' inquiry was called and the race eventually declared void for starting 43 seconds earlier than its scheduled 2pm – thanks to the weighing room clock by which the starter was instructed to set his watch being 90 seconds fast.

1980

Leading jump jockey Andy Turnell visited Perth for two rides in October 1980 – and was soon wishing he hadn't. His first ride, on 3-1 shot Vendevar in a handicap hurdle, saw the pair tail off by halfway. Andy then partnered 11-10 favourite Lazzario in a three-year-old hurdle – in which the horse whipped round at the start, unseating the jockey. The race was won by a local bookie's wife. The locals were not best pleased, and according to the book *100 Years Racing in Scone Palace Park*, the stewards had to 'barricade themselves in the weighing room and phone for police reinforcements'.

It was Turnell's first visit to ride at Perth – he did not return.

1981

Roy Davies won on Milliondollarman at a Worcester meeting in November 1981, followed by Hywel Davies winning on Rogairio, then by Granville Davies winning on Santoss.

1982

Former Cheltenham Gold Cup winner Little Owl was 4-11 favourite for the three-runner Fulwell Chase at Kempton in January 1982. His opponents were 5-2 Venture To Cognac and 66-1 Great Dean. A flurry of straight forecast bets for the second and third favourites appeared, with most bookies reporting large numbers of them.

Little Owl pulled up during the race, as Venture To Cognac beat Great Dean, the forecast paying a hefty £14.27 for a 10p stake. Bookies paid out an estimated £300,000 on the outcome. Stewards interviewed the favourite's jockey and part-owner Jim Wilson, recording his explanation that he was unable to steer his mount properly after the bit had come out of his mouth, so pulled him up.

Bookies' organisation BOLA staged an investigation, concluding, 'There is no reason to withhold payment.'

1982

The first 'timber' race at a major US track was run at Arlington Park on the track's Budweiser Million Day, with William Chewning riding Shy Donald to victory in the $15,000 event – the largest prize ever offered for a 'timber' race. Described as 'America's version of the steeplechase' in a *60 Minutes* feature, timber racing was explained as 'a distinctly blue-blooded pursuit, distantly related to the far-off days when horsemen raced through the countryside jumping hedges along the way. Instead of navigating over large brush hurdles, runners and riders jump fixed wooden rail fences.'

1983

The *Sporting Chronicle* racing newspaper ceased publication on 23 July 1983, having first been published in 1871. From a peak circulation of 120,000 per day, it dwindled to an unsustainable 33,000.

1984

Steve Smith Eccles' riding of Green Dolphin in a Uttoxeter chase in October 1984 was rubbish, decided one punter – or else why did he throw a dustbin at the jockey and his horse, during the race? They didn't win.

1985

Perth's September meeting was abandoned, with clerk of the course David McHarg observing, 'Any going that's visible is heavy, the rest is under water.'

During the same month, bookie John Lovell permitted his Cardiff betting shop to be used for a wake, celebrating his long-time customer Jimmy Peters. 'It's the way he would have wanted to go – he spent most of his life in betting shops,' added Lovell.

1986

It was 58th time lucky for Alf Rubin in October 1986 as the *Morning Star* tipster selected 4/9 Suhailie, winner of a three-runner race to break his sequence of 57 consecutive losers.

1987

Sue Thompson won the 100th running of the annual Wellington Steeplechase in New Zealand, becoming the first female rider to win a premier jump race in that country.

1988

Mourners listening to the Rev Bob White at the funeral of their friend Bill Brown in 1988 were shocked when he told them Bill wanted them all to back a horse for him – Grey General, running that afternoon in the 2.30pm at Wolverhampton. They had a whip-round and backed the horse at 4-1. It won and Bill's brother Jack said, 'He just wanted to make his friends happy for the last time.'

1988

Princess Anne rode a US winner, partnering Wood Chisel to win a flat race for amateurs at the Royal Chase meeting in Nashville.

1989

No starting prices were returned for the 14-runner 1m handicap at Southwell in November 1989. SP reporters explained that only one bookie displayed a full list of odds, so no market was formed. Winner, Admiralty Way, paid £9.80 on the tote.

1990

For the first time in Britain all of the runners in a race – four of them – were supplemented entries after all the entries for Doncaster's *Racing Post* Trophy were withdrawn. Steve Cauthen won in late October 1990 on 2-1 favourite Peter Davies.

1991

Awaiting the outcome of a three-way photo finish at Lingfield in December 1991, Leonard Seale, the owner of eventual 11-4 winner Super Sally, collapsed and died of a heart attack without hearing the result.

1991

The Queen reportedly made a killing on the outcome of the Derby as 'she won £16, courtesy of Generous', reported the *Daily Mail*, adding, 'She apparently jumped with glee.'

1992

'I told the Queen a horseracing joke and I was off and running,' recalled legendary portrait photographer Terry O'Neill of how he put Her Majesty at her ease when he photographed her in 1992.

1993

Trainer Martin Pipe's wife Carol was with him at Taunton in 1993 when their Elite Reg's tongue strap went missing. Carol dashed to the ladies' toilets and removed her tights – which were then used to hold down their runner's tongue. The horse was pulled up in the race.

1994

Riding on the point-to-point course at Penshurst in 1994, to undertake the serious business of scattering a friend's ashes there, Stan Luckhurst did so with due ceremony – at least, until the unfortunate point at which his horse was spooked, immediately parting company with the luckless Luckhurst, who fell straight into the ashy remnants of his late pal.

1995

Blythe Miller, who became the US's first female champion steeplechase jockey in 1994, repeated the feat this year.

1996

Irish jockey and trainer Phil Canty, born in 1918, died in December of this year. His father James, though overshadowed as a jockey by his brother Joe, trained, sending out Mondragon to win the 1939 Irish Derby, ridden by seven-time Irish champion jockey Joe.

Phil had success under both codes, and rode two Irish Classic winners: the 1950 Irish St Leger on Morning Madam and the 1955 Irish 1,000 Guineas on Sir Winston Churchill's filly Dark Issue. His last British winner was on Anne Biddle's three-year-old Islam in the Royal Caledonian Hunt Cup at Edinburgh on 18 September 1962.

Racing writer Marcus Armytage wrote in his 2005 book *Hot Cherry* that Phil, 'Was as famous for the winners he rode as he was for the non-triers he, to coin a currently popular euphemism, "never placed to challenge". One day, after he finished third in a five-horse race, his trainer asked, "What do you think, Canty?"

'"Well sir," he replied, "I'd have no trouble beating the two in front, but I'm not sure about the two behind."'

When James Canty retired from training in the mid-1960s, Phil succeeded him at the Curragh and upheld the family tradition by becoming successful in that discipline.

1997

'I hope she finds the whole thing funny,' declared racing fan John Milton optimistically in November 1997 after naming the race he sponsored at Newton Abbot in honour of his ex-wife, the She's Finally Gone Handicap Hurdle.

1998

The Wild Goose Chase, a flat race open to jockeys who had ridden in the Grand National Steeplechase in Maryland, USA, prior to 1990, attracted a field including 78-year-old Kingdom Gould, and ten-time national winner Charlie Fenwick, but was won by a mere stripling, 62-year-old Irv Naylor on Tarsky.

1999

A little-known jockey sporting bright yellow hair to show support for a fundraising effort for stricken fellow rider Scott Taylor gave Edmond an enterprising pillar-to-post front-running ride to win the Welsh Grand National. That man, Richard Johnson, would end up as a multiple champion jump jockey. Sadly, Taylor was never able to ride again.

2000

For the first time, a Scandinavian horse lined up in the Grand National. Trained by Rune Haugen, hopes were high that 100-1 Trinitro's appearance, partnered by Robert Bellamy, may attract even more runners from this part of the world. However, the horse's departure at the first fence – four others fell at this obstacle, as well – may have deterred any others thinking of having a go.

2002

In 2002 a London vicar, the Rev Nicholas Wheeler, conducted a service in a William Hill betting shop in Camden, which stood on the site of the original St Michael with All Saints and St Thomas Church. To commemorate the church's 125th anniversary the Rev held a service among the shop's usual business of the day – although he did turn down your author's offer of a free £125 bet, with any proceeds to go towards church funds.

A few years before this incident Lord Runcie, Archbishop of Canterbury from 1980 to 1991, had met Hill's managing director of the day, John Brown, at a charity dinner in York, and told him he fancied a flutter on a horse he'd seen with an 'ecclesiastical name', so John had opened probably the only account they'd ever held for an Archbishop of Canterbury. There was no divine intervention – the horse lost.

2004

Guy Willoughby rode his first winner under rules, Inn From The Cold, at Carlisle, in November 2004, before returning to his job as an explosives expert. His winner's trainer, Len Lungo, noted, 'Guy may not be the best amateur around, but I assure you he is better at riding than I am at bomb disposal.'

2006

An international news agency reported that in October of this year, 'A wild bear attacked three race horses on a practice run near the town of Ransäter, in central Sweden, but was forced to retreat into the forest with a broken leg and a bruised ego.'

2008

Jockey John Egan was fined AU\$8,000 – then £3,340 – in November 2008, for calling two vets inspecting his Melbourne Cup mount, Yellowstone, 'a couple of tinpot Hitlers'.

2009

Mick Channon-trained Youmzain completed a hat-trick of seconds in the Prix de l'Arc de Triomphe in 2009 – having finished in the same position in both 2007 and 2008.

2011

In November 2011, a British Sunday newspaper reported that four racecourses – Doncaster, Epsom, Pontefract and Windsor – had become, as the *Racing Post* put it, 'hotbeds' for 'dogging'. In the interests of accuracy, added *Racing Post*, it had 'checked a number of websites devoted to the pastime and was shocked to find this was no tabloid fabrication'.

2012

Having won the Zimbabwe Derby two years earlier, but now no longer actively racing, Winter's Night arrived in South Africa to take up a new equine career – joining a group of four retired ex-race horses now used on patrols in a 3,500-acre private reserve in the Kruger National Park, to protect rhino, giraffe and other wildlife. The new role involved carrying guards there to deter potential poachers, to spot snares and follow intruders' tracks. One of the riders utilising Winter's Night was Anna Mussi, who had trained at the British Racing School in Newmarket and worked for trainer Ian Williams.

2015

Born in 1985, the youngest of ten siblings, Michelle Payne had predicted at the age of seven that she would win the Melbourne Cup as a jockey. She duly fulfilled the boast this year on Prince Of Penzance for trainer Darren Weir.

2019

The 2019 Magnolia Cup, a charity race staged at the Glorious Goodwood meeting, saw a unique achievement by 18-year-old student Khadija Mellah, who rode the Charlie Fellowes-trained Haverland to victory, in the process becoming the first rider to win a British race wearing a hijab. In 2022 the race became the first before which all of the jockeys taking part took to the knee.

2020

Hexham missed out on celebrating 130 years of racing at the course on Monday, 20 April 2020, with its anniversary card falling victim to jump racing's suspension because of the Covid-19 pandemic.

2021

Trainer Kim Bailey told *Daily Telegraph* writer Rick Broadbent how upset punters can become if one of his – and probably most other trainers – horses under-performs. He told Broadbent that in March 2021, after one of his horses had failed to win, he received an email, reading, 'You want to hope I don't find out where you and that f***ing scumbag David Bass [jockey] live. Smash a baseball bat over your heads!'

2022

It was reported in late May 2022 on *Racing Post*'s website, 'A New York-bred stakes winner who sold for $150,000 at Keeneland as a broodmare prospect is actually a male, according to a lawsuit pending in Lexington, Kentucky.'

The horse in question, named Kept True, had gone through the Keeneland January 2021 Horses of All Ages Sale, and was purchased as a five-year-old broodmare prospect.

Kept True had five wins, two seconds, and two thirds from 14 starts to, er, his/her credit, and prize money of $323,659 running against females.

Crawford Farms took possession of Kept True without having the horse examined by their own vet, only to reportedly discover, via examinations and tests, that Kept True is a mare 'in outward appearance only'.

AlphaBetical

AUSSIE ANTICS

'He bets the Charlie at the Fireman's, the Froth at the Chocolates and Away at the Redders,' was a sentence uttered by an Aussie bookie and reported by Ned Wallish in his 1989 *Dictionary of Slang* book, which vividly illustrated how Aussies and Brits are divided by the same language.

Wallish went on to explain that 'Charlies' was short for 'Charlie Chase', an obscure American comedian whose name became rhyming slang for 'place'. 'Fireman's' references top racecourse bookmaker Eddie Birchley, previously a member of the Brisbane Fire Department. 'Froth' is rhyming slang for 'double', as in 'froth and bubble'; 'the chocolates' as for 'chocolate frogs', aka 'dogs'; 'away' is a bookmaker taking bets from venues other than where he is physically working; 'Redders' is a derogatory term for 'harness racing' or 'trots' from 'Red Hots'.

Other terms Wallish explained included 'angora' for the tote, from angora goat, 'autumn leaves' is a jump jockey suffering a succession of falls; 'doctor' is a bookie reluctant to take serious bets, suggesting the punter could 'get better' odds elsewhere; 'hoop' is a jockey; 'lobster' a $20 note; 'squeeze box' is trap five in a dog race; 'undertaker' is a bookmaker known for actively soliciting bets for horses he believes to be non-triers; 'washy' is a horse sweating up pre-race.

BEATEN BROADSWORD

On 30 August 2022, three-year-old Broadspear scuppered tens of thousands of accumulative bets by being beaten at odds of 1-16 at Chepstow, thus becoming one of the shortest-priced beaten favourites ever recorded in British racing history. 11-2 Painless Potter won the race. The hottest-ever beaten favourite in Britain is 1-25 Royal Forest, who lost at Ascot back in 1948.

BETTING SHOPS

'Where you pay money to guess wrong,' wrote columnist Guy Browning in the *Guardian Weekend*, in August 2005.

BOOKMAKERS

Bookmakers in South Africa were originally known as 'pencillers', 'metallicians', 'fielders', and 'the leather-lunged fraternity'.

CAN'T SPELL, WON'T SPELL?

Keen to help promote a race being run at Kempton in May 1996, in aid of an establishment for dyslexics, William Hill advertised odds for the runners in the *Racing Post* under the heading, 'Dyslexia Instititutite Handicap'.

DEAD CERT

In 2008 when working for William Hill, I arranged for the payout of £42,000 in winnings to the relatives of a deceased punter, who had sat on the cheque he had originally received without cashing it for ten years. By that time, the bank refused to honour it.

ENDER'S BEGINNER

Kieran Schofield and 50-1 joint-eighth favourite of the nine Beverley runners romped to an 18-length lead in a one and a half mile handicap, in June, 2022 – somehow hanging on for a three-quarter length victory – the first on the flat for the trainer, Sara Ender, who described the five-year-old as 'lazy, never works very well – this was going to be his last run before retirement.' Next time out he finished last of nine.

EXPERT OPINIONS

They are great, and often useful – but they can go wrong, too. Just ask top jockey John Francome who, when previewing the 1996 Grand National on TV programme *The Morning Line*, advised viewers, 'You can scrub him out. He would need to travel in a horse box to get the trip,' when discussing Rough Quest, the 7-1 favourite, who won under Mick Fitzgerald.

And the following year, respected tipster Mark 'Couch' Winstanley, declared that Lord Gyllene 'has as much chance of success as Ginger Spice joining a convent'. Lord Gyllene won by 25 lengths at 14-1.

They're not all bad, though – ask broadcaster John Inverdale, who, at the 1990 Cheltenham Festival, was tipped 100-1 Gold Cup winner Norton's Coin, by Richard Pitman, former jockey and also husband of trainer Jenny.

Or the then William Hill chief executive David Harding, who in September 2005 'credited' *Racing Post* tipster 'Pricewise' with denting the company's profits following a ten-week winning streak, saying their accounts 'could have been a lot better, and would have been, if it wasn't for Pricewise'.

FOR PETE'S SAKE

Peter Lancaster loved a bet. After he died, aged 80, in December 2021, relatives released a balloon in his memory on Father's Day, in June 2022 – it was found outside his local William Hill shop in Chorley, Lancashire, where he used to work.

FRANKLY AMAZING

Veteran US trainer Frank Passero ran up a 7,000,000-1 sequence of 14 consecutive winners at Gulfstream Park, USA, starting on 24 January 1996.

GLOVELY GAMBLES

British-organised racing festivals in Shanghai during the 1850s and 1860s were popular with females, although fashionable etiquette of the day precluded ladies from using cash with which to gamble. 'They started wagering gloves instead,' recorded author Austin Coates in his book *China Races*, 'and by 1860 they were wagering all kinds of things – bonnets, hats, cigar boxes, fans, even umbrellas. At the spring meeting of 1861 a husband was overheard restricting his wife to wagers of ten dozen gloves.'

GULLY GULLY

An early 20th century racecourse tipster, described by veteran bookie Sammy Nixon in 2005, 'Dressed up in a black cloak as a wizard. He would have an apple in his mitts and suddenly it would disappear and come back cut in half with a tip for the next race in it.'

HORARY NUMEROLOGY

This is not a term with which I was familiar until I stumbled across Indian author Rasajo's 1972 fascinating book *Horary Numerology of the Turf*, in which he 'places before racing enthusiasts his 25 years of research and close study of planetary influence on numbers as applicable to horse and dog racing. The system is universal and can be used in any part of the world.'

I found it as, er, useful, as following the racing tips once featured in the *Daily* and *Sunday Sport* newspapers which were relayed to readers from long-deceased champion jockey Fred Archer, via psychic Doris Bulwark.

MADAME X

She was known initially as 'The Mysterious Madame X' when she launched a financial assault on Australian bookmakers in the early 1920s, following the sudden death of her own bookie husband.

Later revealed to be Maude Vandenberg, she began betting on a large scale at the racecourses, particularly following Amounis. When that horse contested the 1929 Cantala Stakes at Flemington she approached Jim Hackett, leading layer of the day, and asked for £2,000 at odds of 7-2. Hackett took the bet, so she asked for the same again. He took it. She asked again. He took it. After the race she was £21,000 better off.

Still following Amounis, she teamed up with fellow punter Eric Connolly to back the horse and Phar Lap to land the Caulfield Cup-Melbourne Cup double, which was being offered at 50-1 by flamboyant bookie Andy 'the Coogee Bunny' Kerr. They hit him for six figures.

Vandenberg finally quit the racing scene, taking with her an estimated £150,000 profit from the ring.

POWERFUL PROFIT

Leuven Power landed a £60,000 bet at odds of 5-6 – so £50,000 profit – with *Star Sports* when returning from a 302-day lay-off, to win at Salisbury on 9 July 2022.

QUEEN CONQUERED

Queen Elizabeth II's horse, Constitution, was backed down to 5-6 favourite in a Ffos Las six-furlong sprint in July 2022, but finished last of 13, as 125-1 Once More For Luck won.

RUTHLESS JERRY

Uttoxeter's £75,000 bet365 Summer Cup in June 2022 saw 33-1 Jerrysback beat 50-1 Ruthless Article, the two longest-odds runners of the 16.

ST PAUL'S CATHEDRAL

The St Paul's Cathedral Dean officially opened a new betting shop at Old Bailey, London, on 11 January 1991.

STRANGE WINNER

Living in the appropriately name Betton Grange in Shropshire, David Gough lashed out 5p on a six-horse accumulator in March 1986 – which landed him winning odds of 1,648,959-1 and a return from Coral of £82,521.

SWINGER

As Royal Ascot got under way in 2008, the tote launched their new 'Swinger' bet, which occasioned a few risqué remarks. The bet required punters to nominate two horses to finish in the first three.

THAT WAS THE PLAN!

Rectory Oak was a 999-1 chance coming to the last at Newton Abbot in July 2022, with two leaders up ahead, well clear, only for both to capsize at the last fence. 'It was never in doubt,' joked jockey Brendan Powell.

'THUGS, MONEY LAUNDERERS AND DRUG DEALERS'

Anita Graham, the 2004 Betting Shop Manager of the Year, was upset by media depiction of bookies and betting shop staff. She said, 'I've written to *Eastenders* to complain about how we are portrayed. We're thugs, money launderers and drug dealers, It's a travesty. They can't even count on TV – I saw a £100 bet at 50-1 paid out as £5,000. What happened to the £100 stake money?'

TIPSTERS

A subject well-known to any regular punter. In June 2008, somewhat bizarrely, the Office of Fair Trading launched a campaign to protect punters from wasting money on iffy tipsters. But they didn't seem to consider the philosophical question of the morality of people happy to accept the possibility of making money from potentially illegal methods – well, until, that is, such time as they realise that they themselves have been deceived. At which point they may demand that someone else should get their money back for them. Punter Beware is probably the safest philosophy to follow.

ZAFAR ZO GOOD

Sisters Abbie and Ella McCain made light of having only one ride each at different meetings on Wednesday, 14 July 2021, to conjure a family day to cherish when their mounts won at combined odds of 132-1. Both winners were trained by the pair's father, Donald, and even mother Sian got in on the act as her colours were carried to victory by Abbie at Uttoxeter on 6-1 Zafar, a horse they bought together at the horses-in-training sales in May. Ella McCain followed her older sister's example, winning on her only ride of the day when front-running 18-1 Russco claimed division one of the 7f handicap at Wolverhampton. Ella, 20, and Abbie, 21, are granddaughters of the late Ginger McCain, the legendary trainer of three-time Grand National winner Red Rum.

Dodgy Dealing

1718

It was reported that Crutches had started as a hot favourite to win 'the Plate' at York, but that jockey Thomas Duck clearly was under orders not to win, so, 'finding his horse winning, in spite of all his efforts to stop him, with courage worthy of a better cause, threw himself off when leading at the distance post'.

1751

Two of the finest horses of the day were matched against each other at the Curragh in Ireland in September 1751, when Sir Ralph Gore's Black and All Black took on the Earl of March's Bazajet for a stake of 10,000gns over a 4m distance.

Bazajet was made favourite but, stated a witness account, 'To the joy of a great number of spectators, Sir Ralph's horse came in about ten yards before the other.'

However, this was far from the end of the drama, and it then transpired, according to the book *Life of Old Q*, about March – whose nickname was Old Q – 'The jockey who rode Lord March's horse was of a lighter weight than he who rode the Irishman's champion, therefore recourse had to be made to the usual "loadings", with a shotted belt.'

However, it was also reported, 'During the progress of the match the encumbered jockey managed to get rid of his burden, which was picked up by a careful observer and adroitly slipped by him into the jockey's jacket on returning to scale.'

But the illegal move was noted when 'the quick visual organs of the Celtic duellist caught sight of this act of racing ledgerdemain, and with typical impetuosity he seized Lord March's representative by the shoulder and threatened to thrash him on the spot if he did not at once acknowledge his guilt, as well as at whose instigation he had acted'.

The frightened rider promptly owned up and 'cast the vile reproach' upon his master.

Unimpressed by March's reaction when charged with cheating, Gore, 'Despatched the following note to the lord, "My lord, I shall be happy to meet you by five o'clock tomorrow morning at … and if your lordship will have the goodness to bring a friend, a surgeon and a case of pistols with you, I doubt not but our little misunderstanding will be settled in less than five minutes."'

With 'a punctuality worthy of a better cause, Lord March appeared on the ground, accompanied by a second, surgeon and other adjuncts to an exit from the world'.

Gore also arrived, 'With a like retinue of his own, but increased by a polished oak coffin, which, "sans ceremonie", he deposited on the ground, end up, with its lid facing Lord March. Surprise gave way to terror when his lordship read the inscription plate engraved with his own name and title, and the date and year of his demise, which was the actual day, as yet scarcely warm!'

The Irishman then announced, 'My dear fellow, you are of course aware that I never miss my man; and as I find myself in excellent trim for sport this morning, I have not a shadow of doubt that this oaken box will shortly be better calculated for you than your present dress.'

Lord March at once made a full and complete apology to his opponent – which was graciously accepted.

1848

The final meeting held at Oswestry in 1848 ended with disputes on the course. Maid of Lymme, ridden by Anthony Clarke, finished first in the Sir Watkin Cup only to be disqualified for carrying 3lb extra weight. The second contretemps was about the £50 Town Subscription Plate, a three-runner race which, declared the *Eddowes Journal*, was fixed – 'that the "chisel" was at work, no one could entertain a doubt'. The prize money was withheld.

1857

The Earl of Derby wrote to the Jockey Club, noting, 'It has become a subject of general observation and regret that the number of men of station and fortune who support the Turf is gradually diminishing, and that an increasing proportion of persons in an inferior position, who keep them not for the purpose of sport but as mere instruments of gambling.

'I venture to think that it is your duty to exercise a wholesome influence upon the character and respectability of the Turf.

'You cannot debar any man from keeping race horses, but when among their number are found those against whom flagrant cases of disgraceful fraud and dishonesty have been legally established, it appears to me clearly within your province to stamp them with your reprobation, and to exclude them from association, on an equal footing, with the more honourable supporters of the Turf.'

1864

The *Sporting Gazette* was not happy at the conduct of a meeting at Perth, with its racing correspondent writing that it was 'very deficient in legitimate racing, the fields being extremely small and, as a matter of course, a considerable amount of "squaring" took place, and unless there is some great change in the management we have seen the last of bona fide racing at Perth'.

1896

A pair of Americans decided to bring a squad of horses over from the States to target British races, and did so in the early part of this year. Mr W. Duke Jr and Mr E. Wishard brought over a squad of ten potential runners, four of which already had winning form to their names. They were to be based and trained at the Red House in Newmarket. Their first runner, six-year-old Helen Nichols, finished second at Newmarket in the 'green with white shoulder-straps' silks of the setup. Their next, George H. Ketcham, was also a runner-up at Newmarket, and they broke their duck when the appropriately named Wishard won the ten-runner Wilton Handicap at Manchester at 8-1. Helen Nichols then won on Derby day at Epsom at 100-8 while Wishard followed up by beating an odds-on favourite to win at Ascot at 100-12 in the Queen's Stand Plate.

They landed four winners at the Newmarket First July Meeting, with American jockey Lester Reiff becoming well-known as a result, although he slightly blotted his copybook as he rode Wishard in the Hare Park Handicap, looking all over the winner until he mistook the winning post and eased up too early and was overtaken, but he made amends by winning the opening race of the second day on 6-1 George H. Ketcham.

Returning to the US at the end of the successful season, Duke commented, 'We did right well, and that in spite of the handicappers, who didn't often give us a chance. We shall come back next winter, I hope.'

Six of the horses were sold off to British buyers for a total of 7,370gns – 'very far in excess of what they would have sold for in America,' reported *Racing Illustrated*.

The whole episode looked to be something of a fairytale achievement, but some had their doubts.

Reiff had already been suspended for throwing races in the States, where he was barred from horseracing in late 1894 and the early months of 1895.

In May 1894 in the US, Reiff was beaten on a horse called Watterson in suspicious circumstances, a day or two before riding the same horse to victory, causing the *New York Times* on 29 May to declare in stern tones, 'It would be a good thing if the stewards would set the scalpel at work and cut deep enough to find out who was responsible for Reiff's performance. There was certainly someone back of him that was responsible for the jobbery, if jobbery there was. The owners and trainers ought, if guilty, to be hauled over the coals. They are the ones deserving of punishment more than the lad, who is probably simply the tool of the gang that manipulated the job.'

Reiff became champion jockey in the UK in 1900 but had a chequered career, with allegations of race-fixing dogging him, while he and younger brother John would be accused of involvement in a horse doping ring, along with Enoch Wishard and other American gamblers.

While using performance-enhancing stimulants was illegal in the US, it was not outlawed in the UK until 1904.

In October 1901, Reiff and his younger brother John – who had become known as 'Knickerbocker' because of his preferred mode of dress – were reprimanded by the Jockey Club for alleged race-fixing, following an incident at Manchester on 27 September in which Lester's horse, De Lacy, finished second by a head to Minnie Dee, ridden by John. The local stewards were unsatisfied by the brothers' explanations and so referred the matter to the Jockey Club.

Lester's licence was revoked for the 1902 season due to such incidents and he was barred or 'warned off' from racing in other countries, perhaps somewhat throwing suspicion on the success of the American experiment.

John Reiff went on to win the Derby in 1907 and 1912 on Orby and Tagalie, also finishing first on Craganour but being disqualified in favour of 100-1 Aboyeur in 1913.

1903

Warning-off became the penalty, 'If any person shall administer or cause to be administered, for the purpose of affecting the speed of a horse, drugs or stimulants internally, by hypodermic or other method.'

1912

At a meeting in Tapanui, New Zealand, in 1877, the stewards disqualified a horse who had 'glaringly been pulled'. A newspaper report at the time declared quite unbelievably, 'It was that obvious that some punters refused to collect their dividend on the winner.'

1915

Steward Frank McGill had heard that jockey Jimmy Dunne, riding Soldier Lad at Springsure, Australia, 'was not off'. So he rode over on his own horse to keep a close eye on the race and, sure enough, Dunne 'accidentally' fell from his mount, whereupon McGill rode over to the floored rider, laying on the ground, and issued him with a 12-month suspension.

1919

It transpired that the two-year-old Coat of Mail, who won Stockton's Faceby Plate during the autumn, was actually a three-year-old named Jazz. And in December of this year Silver Badge won a selling hurdle, before being revealed as the much higher quality Shining More. The run of 'ringers' carried on in 1920 as Golden Plate, a two-year-old running at Chester, turned out to be three-year-old Homs. Investigations resulted in six people being 'warned off' and the three 'real' horses 'perpetually disqualified'. However, such deceptions had clearly been happening on the turf for many years as an 1838 letter to the Jockey Club had claimed, 'Horses being permitted to race in other names ... has lately been carried on to a great extent, and deeply to the public prejudice.'

1922

In an effort to defeat the forging of totalisator tickets, New Zealand's Napier Park Racing Club subjected 'winning' tickets to an 'acid test'. Those turning pink were paid out on.

1948

Presumably designed to prevent dodgy dealings, in late 1948 over 30,000 sets of fingerprints, ranging from those of grooms to high-ranking racing officials, were taken by the United States Thoroughbred Protective Racing Bureau, 'as a step towards protecting racing and its public'. Declared Spencer J. Drayton, organiser of the bureau, 'It is gratifying to note the willing response of racing's personnel.'

1950s

Kiwi racing was rocked in the early 1950s when the exposure of a race-rigging ring resulted in the disqualification for life of two jockeys – Don Mackinnon and Reg Collett. Two more were banned for three years each and a trainer suspended for five years.

1968

The first Kentucky Derby disqualification took place as testing on first past the post Dancer's Image revealed an illegal medication, so runner-up Forward Pass was declared the winner. Cue five years of ultimately fruitless court action by Dancer's Image's team.

1992

Some people have a conscience – like the person who in autumn 1992 sent an anonymous letter containing a £50 note to William Hill's Customer Relations Department. He described himself as 'Guilty Conscience' and explained, 'In 1984 I placed a yankee bet in one of your shops in Chelsea. I handed in a £50 note and was given 19 fivers and four pound coins. I have realised the lady who made that mistake had to answer for that mistake. I visited the shop to put my dishonesty right but the staff had changed. All I can do is ask you to accept this £50 note and my apologies.' The money was donated by William Hill to a racing charity.

1993

Tony Ryan was jailed for five years after disguising himself by covering his face with tights before stealing £332 at gunpoint from terrified staff at a Birmingham betting shop. Not only had this dangerous dunce not noticed that the tights were laddered, giving staff a glimpse of his face, but when making his getaway he dropped a betting slip, on which was written his name and address.

2007

I was in Morocco to see their Derby being run at Souissi. It was the year in which Frankie Dettori had won the English, French and Italian Derbies, so it was a relief to realise by dint of not being here, Frankie wouldn't win this one.

I don't really remember what did win it, but it was the last race of the day which showed me a previously unknown betting scam. The group I was with heard that one of the runners in the final event was owned by a member of the Moroccan royal family, so deduced it must be a cert of the highest order, and plunged their cash on with the tote – there were no bookies at the meeting.

The royal horse, Rubiszo, duly obliged. Celebrations broke out as my fellow racegoers waited to cash in their winning tickets to the tote operator, who had told our group that calculations would take a few minutes and had gone to check on just how long. It soon became more than a few minutes.

Eventually he returned, and began paying out to the winners in our group, who were returning from the tote with baffled expressions. 'He's just given us our money back,' complained one. Then another. Then, all of them.

The tour leader went to see what had happened. Had the race been voided, perhaps? If that were the case, then clearly even those who had backed a loser should get their money back?

As my companions realised this, they also noticed that our tote man had done a runner. All of a sudden no one at the course could speak English – and our coach was revving up ready to transport us back to our hotel. There was no option but to get on the coach and accept that any winnings had clearly been 'donated' to the tote operator who had at least given stake money back to the gullible tourists who thought they'd landed a winner.

2022

'There will no doubt be a buzz in the air at Saturday's big meetings at Cheltenham and Doncaster,' reported Jack Keene in *The Sun* on 28 January 2022.

The buzz to which he was referring came from a team of drones hovering overhead beaming live pictures to in-running gamblers looking to achieve a decisive advantage over their rivals, which some considered to be if not strictly illegal, certainly stretching the rules extremely thinly.

The airborne devices had been causing racecourses a headache – but drone operators were cashing in.

A pro punter quoted in the story alleged there were up to six 'firms' of drone operators coining it in across the country – one even reportedly paying to operate from an elderly woman's back garden near Chelmsford City racecourse.

Punters wanting access to the near-instant pictures provided by the drones were being charged up to £60 per meeting – but in return being handed a huge advantage on the in-running markets.

If 150 to 200 punters bought into the service at even a quiet midweek meeting that could bring in up to £10,000 per fixture for the drone gang.

Punters buying into the currently legal service were gaining a crucial edge over TV racing viewers – of around a second on Racing TV viewers and up to four or five over Sky Sports Racing and ITV.

Racecourses believe their media rights are infringed by the drones beaming live pictures to punters.

Some courses were renting boxes to in-running punters for substantial income, but many of those bettors started using drone pictures, feeling those viewing instant footage have an advantage with bird's-eye-view angles.

There is also a constant risk of a drone crash, such as one near Chepstow racecourse during its Welsh National meeting, possibly even causing injury to horses, jockeys or racegoers.

There have been examples reported of police being called, and drone pilots fleeing – or proving they are properly licensed.

Arena Racing Company – with 16 racecourses in Britain – said drones were an 'ongoing problem'. Yet, thus far, no legal proceedings had taken place.

Vintage Racing Glossary

All definitions below are taken from the 1948 *Racing Review* magazine.

ARMSTRONG, Captain, or 'Johnny'
A rider suspected of pulling a horse, or not letting it do its best in a race is said to be 'Doing the Captain [or 'J.'] Armstrong.'

ASKING THE ODDS
When the betting on a horse is 'odds-on' it is said that the bookmaker is 'asking [the] odds'.

'BACK TEETH PULLED OUT'
Said to have been done to a horse if the rider is suspected of preventing its winning.

BOTH WAYS
Earlier term for 'each way'.

COLOURS, Sending in
A jockey is said to 'send in his colours' when he terminates for any reason an engagement to ride the horses of a certain owner.

COSH
Alternative name for 'whip'.

HEAVIES
A horse is said to be 'running in heavies' when it has not been specially shod with plates for a race.

KID
An apprentice jockey.

ON THE RIBS
Stony broke, or lost all one's money.

PENCILLER
A bookmaker operating on the dividing line between Tattersall's and the Members' Enclosure. One who caters for the elite of the betting world and accepts commissions on the spoken word.

SELLINGER
Slang term for the St Leger Classic race.

SPIVS
Hangers-on of the racecourse, attending most meetings and preying on generosity of racegoers.

TAPES, The
Rubber strands of the starting gate, raised mechanically when the starter pulls a lever.

TOUT
One who watches race horses in their training, finds out information and reports it, usually to the press. Adds the glossary, 'Previously this was a despised occupation and much disliked by all, but now recognised as a skilled and honourable profession, receiving all reasonable assistance from most trainers.'

TUBED
Horse which has 'gone in its wind' and undergone a tracheotomy operation to assist its breathing.

TWITCH
A contrivance of a string loop and a stick with which the upper lip of a horse's mouth is held to facilitate the administration of medicine or, in the case of a difficult horse, shoeing or other operations.

WARNED OFF
Debarred from racecourse and race meetings as a result of being involved in, or causing, corrupt practices.

WIDE BOYS
Hangers-on of racing, living on their wits and little else.

Nicknames

'Boots' and 'Slippers'
Niall 'Slippers' Madden, an Irish jockey who won the 2006 Grand National on Numbersixvalverde. Madden's nickname became 'Slippers' as a comparison with his jockey father, also Niall, whose nickname had been 'Boots' and who had always had ambitions of winning the National in which he first rode in 1978, falling on So, and did so again in his next two attempts on Kilkiwell (1981) and Gandy VI (1982). Attitude Adjuster got him round three times, finishing eighth, fifth and 12th from 1987 to 1989.

'Choc'
Trainer David Nicholson came up with the 'Choc' tag for jockey Robert Thornton who, when he arrived at his Cotswolds stables straight from school, had a diet which seemed to consist of nothing but chocolate. His biggest wins in the saddle came for long-time boss Alan King in the Champion Hurdle, Champion Chase and Stayers' Hurdle. Of course, there is also a connection with the name of Thorntons Confectionery.

'Choirboy'
Walter Swinburn was a fresh-faced 19-year-old when he rode Shergar to win the Derby. His boyish, deceptively innocent-looking features acquired him the nickname of the Choirboy.

'Fiddler'
Newmarket trainer Arthur Goodwill (1911–94), son of a Blackburn hairdresser, turned up to his first day as a stable lad carrying a violin in a case. His daughter Linda was champion female rider in 1973, winning four times on his Pee Mai.

'The Head Waiter'
Harry Wragg (1902–85) who, as a jockey, had 13 Classic victories to his credit, plus a further five as a trainer, was so-named because of his favourite 'come from behind' late challenge tactics.

'Himself'
The great chaser Arkle began receiving fan mail as his reputation grew, and when some arrived bearing the name and address, 'Himself, Ireland', the nickname caught on.

'Kentucky Kid'
Champion jockey Steve Cauthen, who came to the UK from the US, acquired this odd nickname purely because he came from Kentucky.

'Leglock'

Now a regular member of the *ITV Racing* team, Luke Harvey was a jump jockey for 16 years whose biggest success came on Cool Ground in the 1990 Welsh Grand National. He received his moniker for his rather unique upright style of riding, and owner Terry Warner even named one of his horses Leg Lock Luke.

'Moppy'

Sir Gordon Richards (1904–86) won 14 Classics, and also had several placed horses in Classic races as a trainer. He was known as Moppy because of his thin, black hair.

'The Pocket Hercules'

Jockey Frank Buckle, born in 1776, rode at less than 4st when he began in 1783. He competed until he was 65 and won 27 Classics – the Derby five times, likewise the 2,000 Guineas, six 1,000 Guineas, nine Oaks, and two St Legers. He died in 1832 having had his final mount the year before. He also bred greyhounds, fighting cocks and bulldogs.

'Puppy'

Gold Cup- and Grand National-winning jockey Robbie Power was dubbed 'Puppy' by former jockey Paul Carberry, taking it from popular kids' cartoon Scooby-Doo, whose eponymous canine hero had a nephew called Scrappy, who charged into fights with the battle yelling 'Puppy Power'.

'Old Stoneface'/'The Long Fellow'

Lester Piggott – one because of his craggy visage, the other because of his towering height of 5ft 8in.

'Queen'

Francine Villeneuve, a retired Canadian jockey and racing pioneer, was known by the nickname 'The Queen of Fort Erie' because of a long affiliation with that course, which was also dubbed the 'border oval' because of its proximity to the Canada/USA border. With 1,001 victories and 3,065 combined wins, places and shows, she retired 'for good' in April 2012 as the most successful female Canadian jockey of all time and the first Canadian woman to achieve the 1,000 milestone.

'Red'

John M. Pollard (1909–81) was a Canadian jockey. A founding member of the Jockeys' Guild in 1940, Pollard rode in the US, becoming best known for riding the legendary Seabiscuit. He started out in boxing as 'Cougar' but the flaming nature of his hair led to 'Red' taking over.

'Shark'

According to the Great British Racing website, ITV pundit and former jockey Jason Weaver once, when competing at the international jockeys' challenge in Mauritius, went water skiing with a group of fellow riders and young reporter Matt Chapman. While Chapman was nervously swimming, Weaver dived down and grabbed the inside of his leg. Having thought he had been bitten by a shark, Chapman broke all records to get back to the boat. Weaver's nickname stuck.

'The Tinman'

Great jockey Fred Archer won 21 Classics but died much too young, aged only 29 in 1886, by his own hand. The nickname was a reference to his evident love of money, 'tin' being slang for money in those days.

'Weary Willie'

Bill Williamson was an Australian-born jockey who rode his first winner there in 1937 but came to England where he enjoyed two 1,000 Guineas wins, together with a Prix de l'Arc de Triomphe double, with Vaguley Noble in 1968 and Levmoss the following year. His nickname was probably won as a result of his impassive response to either victory or defeat, although he did have a sleepy-eyed look, laconic nature, dry wit and a slow, measured stride.

Did You Know?

* Paul Nicholls's father, Brian, and grandfather, Frank, were both policemen. Paul also eyed up a rather different career before opting to go into racing, 'I reckon I could have made a decent living as an egg salesman.'

* On the day Pope Benedict XVI flew to the UK in 2010 on a state visit the winner of the 3.10 at Lingfield was hammered in from 7-4 to 11-8 and duly romped home – well, it was called Man Of God. Maybe the punters who got on were playing up their winnings from September 2008 when, in race four at Kempton, horse number four was drawn at four, was 4-1 in the betting, and was ridden by Jimmy Fortune. No, Critical Acclaim didn't come fourth – but it did win.

* A.P. McCoy 'wasn't mad into horses when I was very young. Snooker and football were my big passions,' according to his autobiography, *A.P. McCoy*.

* Kieren Fallon suffered from dyslexia, was a promising young pre-teen boxer, and a useful youth player of hurling.

* Although Mick Fitzgerald called his 2008 autobiography *Better Than Sex*, that was not what he said after winning the 1996 Grand National on Rough Quest. What he actually said to interviewer Des Lynam was, 'After that, Des, you know, even sex is an anti-climax.'

* Trainer Mark Johnston's mother, Mary, stood as a parliamentary candidate for the Scottish National Party in Motherwell and Coatbridge.

* Winston Churchill's grandfather, financier Leonard Jerome, founded the American Jockey Club. The New York racecourse, Jerome Park, opened in 1866, was named after him.

* The nickname which was always applied to London's Alexandra Park racecourse, 'the Frying Pan', was originally coined by multiple champion flat jockey Fred Archer.

* Even in the midst of an attack on Saturday, 17 June 1944 at Caen in France, codenamed Operation Epsom, British troops and officers were able to bet on the outcome of that day's Derby. Historian Catrine Clay wrote in her book about German soldier-turned Manchester City goalkeeper Bert Trautmann, 'They put up boards in the midst of battle listing the runners

and riders and took bets, then listened to the results on the wireless.' The 28-1 shot, Ocean Swell, probably meant that few soldiers backed the winner.

* Ilona Barnett, at time of writing the managing director of Stratford Racecourse, was, as a jumps trainer, something of a nervous watcher when her horse Ocheekobee was running, admitting that she 'stuffs her fingers so far into her ears they cross, screws up her eyes, chants, walks on the spot and performs half tucks'. Asked why, if she was so nervous, she trained, Ilona explained, 'We do it for fun.' Fortunately for her nerves the horse finished its running career in 2011.

* Former champion jump jockey Peter Scudamore, not noted for his heavy metal approach to the sport, claimed to be a huge fan of Guns N' Roses. Well, at least listening to them would take Scu's mind off of the day when he was riding at a Fontwell evening meeting in the mid-1980s, only for his mount, Vistule, to dive unexpectedly off the course, leaving the commentator telling spectators, 'Vistule has run off the track and Peter Scudamore has disappeared into the bushes.'

* In 2009, Seattle artist Kim Graham made herself a pair of 'horsey legs', and then made more to sell. They cost about $1,000 and featured optional spring-loaded hooves.

* Ace jockey Eph Smith's real christian name was, seemingly, Eph, as his 1968 autobiography was issued under that name. There are suggestions that it was Eric, but although one or two sources such as Jockeypedia (which also thinks he was Ephraim rather than Eph) and Wikipedia agree, perhaps the most prestigious, *Biographical Encyclopaedia of British Flat Racing* by the eminent Roger Mortimer, Richard Onslow and Peter Willett, lists him as Eph Eric Smith. Whichever it is, he was definitely born on his mother's birthday in 1915, won the Derby and 2,000 Guineas on Blue Peter in 1939, and the St Leger on Premonition in 1953 and sadly committed suicide in 1972. One of the other top jockeys of the time, Doug Smith, was his younger brother.

* Former prime minister David Cameron's uncle by marriage, Sir William Dugdale, rode in the 1952 Grand National, partnering 100-1 shot Cloncarrig but having to take drastic action to make the weight, calling it 'crucifixion, an absolute bloody nightmare' in his autobiography. Harley Street advice produced medication

which 'made me pee like mad' and advice to eat 'one meal of boiled cabbage' a day. Sir William made 11st 13lb but fell at the fence before Becher's. Cameron was an undergraduate at Oxford along with racing writer Chris McGrath, who recalled, 'I used to subscribe to the *Racing Post* and Cameron would come searching for my copy every time his father had a runner.'

The Queen's Majestic Racing Life

After the death of Her Majesty at the age of 96 was announced during the afternoon of 8 September 2022, evening racing, and the whole of the next day's fixtures, were cancelled.

A statement from the BHA read: 'All of British racing is in mourning today following the passing of Her Majesty The Queen. Her Majesty has been one of the greatest and most influential supporters in the history of horseracing. Her passion for racing and the racehorse shone brightly throughout her life, not only through her close involvement in breeding and racing horses, but in her roles as a patron of the Jockey Club and Thoroughbred Breeders Association, and as the figurehead of Royal Ascot.

'It is right, therefore, that all racing is suspended for today and tomorrow as we begin to grieve Her Majesty's passing and remember her extraordinary life and contribution to our sport and our nation.'

Queen Elizabeth's father, King George VI, had an interest in racing, and had owned his final Classic winner when his home-bred filly Hypericum won the 1,000 Guineas in 1946. Following her father's death on 6 February 1952, Queen Elizabeth II was crowned on 2 June 1953. Four days after the Coronation, her Hyperion colt Aureole, bred by her father, finished second in the Derby behind Pinza, the latter ridden by Gordon – later to become Sir – Richards.

Paying tribute to Her Majesty and her great love of, and support for, racing, Marcus Armytage observed in *The Telegraph* that, 'It is an irony not lost on many within the sport that it took the Queen to preserve the sport of kings.'

Added Armytage: 'Never were the extreme emotions of owning a racehorse more evident than at Ascot in 2013 when Estimate narrowly won the Gold Cup and the Queen became the first reigning monarch to win the race in its 200-year history.'

In the tributes to the Queen, some racing-related memories were quickly revealed. The Metro's Amanda Cable unearthed an early example of her jockeyship: 'The Queen used to gallop down Ascot racecourse early in the morning, before racing started. In 1960, she finished fourth of seven in an unofficial race alongside members of the Royal party.'

Supporting this little-known Ascot habit, Ellie Kelly recalled in *The Telegraph* that: 'In her youth the Queen would gallop up the track at Royal Ascot before the start of each race day, headscarf flying, and no protective helmet, such was her confidence around horses.'

Another anecdote told of an unexpected visit by Her Majesty to one of her trainers: He 'invited her inside for a coffee. The Queen followed and sat down in an untidy room on top of a thick throw designed to protect the sofa from dog hair. When the trainer apologised for the state of the throw, the Queen beamed and said, "Don't worry, it's just like home."'

When the Queen attended Royal Ascot each year, yours truly and colleagues would open a betting market on the colour of hat she would be sporting on different days. In 2017 she appeared wearing a hat complete with silk flowers – which had reputedly been removed from a flowerpot spotted by her dresser, Angela Kelly, and sewn on to the brim. Although the colour of chapeau was clearly occasionally leaked by someone close to the Queen, resulting in a flurry of bets for a particular colour, this quirky market remained particularly popular with the media.

Former champion jockey Willie Carson recalled the Queen's incisive memory: 'You had to be careful what you said, because she would pick you up if you got it wrong about a horse. Her mind was still very, very sharp, and the breeding was right at the forefront of her brain. If you just slipped up and said this horse is out of the wrong mare, she would be straight on you.'

Hayley Turner remembered beating one of Her Majesty's runners at Royal Ascot: 'My first Royal Ascot winner, I beat hers by a neck. She rang Michael Bell – I ride a lot of his horses – and said: "I was very cross to start with, but then I thought, no, very well done. Well done, Hayley." So even though I beat her, she sent on her best wishes, so that was good.'

Katie Jerram-Hunnable, whose yard has housed many of the Queen's retired racehorses, recalled in an interview that she would be invited to bring some of the horses to Windsor Castle to ride them in front of Her Majesty: 'After you ride them for her, she always comes out with a brown paper bag with chopped carrots. For as long as I have known her, she always hand feeds her horse a carrot herself – it's always carrots.'

One of the most bizarre stories involving Her Majesty and racing occurred when Spanish officials delayed handing over the equivalent of £57,000 prize money due after the victory at San Sebastian of her horse Enharmonic in August 1993 – because they said that for tax purposes they needed proof that the monarch was British.

Eventually they paid up in 1994, leaving Her Majesty's racing manager Lord Carnarvon commenting, 'It appears the Spanish authorities wanted proof that the Queen is British – it is really quite amusing.'

The Queen was 19 years old when, on 21 May 1945, she first visited a race meeting – Ascot's Whit Monday card, where she saw Sun Up become the first winner of an Ascot race to be trained by a woman, Florence Nagle, although for 'official' purposes at the time it was listed as being trained by her head lad, R. Brown.

Elizabeth's first runner as an owner was Astrakhan – second in Ascot's Sandwell Stakes on 7 October 1949. Her first winner, and the first for 235 years owned by a Queen of England since Queen Anne's Star, was Monave'en, owned jointly with her mother, which was 3-10 favourite over fences at Fontwell on 10 October 1949.

In 1954, the year in which she first became the country's leading owner by prize money, her Aureole won the King George VI and Queen Elizabeth Stakes, and finished runner-up in the Derby.

She won her first Classic with Carrozza, ridden by Lester Piggott, in the 1957 Oaks and was again leading owner, with 16 horses winning 30 races, worth £62,211. During this season she had her first treble, with Pall Mall, Atlas and Might And Main, at Haydock on 17 May.

In 1977 her purple, gold braid, scarlet sleeves, black velvet cap with gold fringe colours were carried to victory in both the Oaks and the St Leger by Dunfermline.

In 1989 she had her first winner in America when Unknown Quantity, her first runner there for 35 years, won the Grade 1 Arlington Handicap, at 10-1, ridden by Jorge Velasquez, at Arlington International, Chicago.

In 1992 a TV documentary showed footage of the Queen winning the Royal party's Derby sweepstake, pocketing £16 after drawing favourite Generous. She was shown collecting three fivers and a pound coin, asking, deadpan, 'What does one do with these?'

On the 40th anniversary of her Coronation on 2 June 1993, Enharmonic won for her at Epsom under Frankie Dettori at 12-1.

The Queen inadvertently revealed how much racing was always on her mind when, addressing parliament during the Queen's Speech in 2003, she announced, 'My Government will continue to reform the National Hunt,' before correcting herself immediately with the words 'National Health Service'.

A TV documentary in December 2007 showed BA staff preparing to welcome her on board a flight to the Baltic and being told that the *Racing Post* must be provided to her as it was 'essential reading'. And in the same year she visited the Kentucky Derby for the first time, sharing a balcony with Ivana Trump and the President of Latvia.

Her Free Agent won the 2008 Chesham Stakes at Royal Ascot, and in that August her Golden Stream broke the track record for two-year-olds at Newmarket. One of her jumpers, Barber Shop, ran unplaced behind winner Kauto Star in the 2009 Cheltenham Gold Cup.

In 2016 a statue was unveiled, between the Rowley Mile racecourse and the High Street, in Newmarket, marking the Queen's 90th birthday, depicting her standing alongside a mare and foal. The headquarters of the Thoroughbred Breeders' Association, of which the Queen was patron since 1953, is in the town.

As so often, Frankie Dettori summed up the sport's reaction to this great loss simply when he poignantly said, 'I've known Her Majesty for 30 years. We lost our greatest ambassador.'

Bibliography

Adams, John, *Over The Hurdles* (Melbourne Books, 2010)

Armytage, Marcus, *Hot Cherry* (Highdown, 2005)

Bloodstock Breeders' Review (Vol Xix, 1930, 1932, 1967, 1969)

Bourke, Algernon, *History Of White's* (London, 1892)

Cavanough and Day, *Cup Day*

Davies, Paul, *Cartmel Races* (TCR, 2006)

Finnegan, Pat, *Racing At Wingatui 1899–1999* (privately published)

Fisher, George, *Guinness Book of Turf Records* (Guinness Superlatives, 1964)

Fitzgerald, Mick, *Better Than Sex* (Racing Post, 2008)

Frith, W.G.C., *The Royal Calcutta Turf Club* (Royal Calcutta Turf Club, 1976)

Hey, Stan, *An Arm and Four Legs* (Yellow Jersey Press, 1998)

Hogan, John, *The Darwin Cup – 120 Years of Racing in the Northern Territory* (NT Racing Commission, 1993)

Hore, J.P., *History of Newmarket and Annals of the Turf Vol 2* (A.H. Bailly and Co, 1886)

Horse Racing (no author credited, 1863)

Jaffee, Jean, *They Raced To Win* (Struik, 1980)

Laird, Dorothy, *Royal Ascot* (Hodder & Stoughton, 1976)

Lake, Tony, *Guide to Jump Racing 1892 – The Complete Record* (2013)

Lambie, Jamie, *100 Years Racing in Scone Palace Park* (Perth Racecourse, 2008)

Lawrence, Anthony, *The Royal Hong Kong Jockey Club* (RHKJC, 1984)

Lee, Brian, *History of Cardiff Racecourse*, (Cwm Nedd Press, 1980)

Longmore, Andrew, *Fallon: The Biography* (Racing Post, 2009)

McCoy, A.P, *A.P.McCoy My Autobiography* (Orion, 2011)

McEvoy, John, *Great Horse Racing Mysteries* (Eclipse Press, 2000)

Mountier, Mary, *Racing Women of New Zealand* (Daphne Brasell Associates, 1993)

Oliver, W.C.S., *From Then…Till Now* (1986)

Prior, C.M., *The History of the Racing Calendar and Stud-Book* (Sporting Life, 1926)

Racegoer's Encyclopaedia And Diary, 1936–37

Raper, Anthony C., *Days at the Races* (Andover History and Archaeological Society, 2006)

Richardson, Charles, *British Steeplechasing and Racing in Ireland* (London Counties Press Association, 1927)

Rossell, John E., *History of the Maryland Hunt Cup 1894–1954* (The Sporting Press, 1954)

Ruckley, Harry, *Oswestry Racecourse* (Shropshire Books, 1989)

Sergeant, Philip W., *Gamblers All* (Hutchinson & Co, 1951)

Seth-Smith, Willett, and Mortimer, Lawrence, *The History of Steeplechasing* (Michael Joseph, 1966)

Shone, Arthur N., *Wrexham Races: The Forgotten Welsh Racecourse* (Snowy Publications, 1991)

Shuback, Alan, *Global Racing* (DRF Press, 2008)

Simpson, Chris, *A Brief Guide to European Jump Racing* (TCR, 2005)

Slusar, John, *Racecourses Here Today and Gone Tomorrow* (volumes 1-4, www.greyhoundderby.com, 2016)

Smith, Raymond, and Costello, Con, *Peerless Punchestown* (Punchestown Racecourse, 2000)

Sole, Laraine, *Wanganui Jockey Club 1848–1998* (Wanganui Jockey Club, 1999)

Somers, Geoffrey V., *The Royal Hong Kong Jockey Club* (Michael Stevenson, 1975)

Stawell, Jessica, *Burford and Bibury Racecourses.* (Hindsight Of Burford, 2000)

Wallish, Ned, *Dictionary of Racing Slang* (A.C.E., 1989)

Watson, S.J., *Between the Flags* (Figgis, 1969)

Welch, Ned, *Who's Who in Thoroughbred Racing* (Who's Who, 1946)

Williams, Johnny, *Racing for Gold* (Williams Publishers, 1987)

Winants, Peter, *Steeplechasing* (Derrydale Press, 2000)